THE EFFECTIVE EXPERT WITNESS

Proven Strategies for Successful Court Testimony

THE EFFECTIVE EXPERT WITNESS

Proven Strategies for Successful Court Testimony

Dr. Robert A. Warren

Gaynor Publishing
Lightfoot, Va. 23090

Copyright © 1997 Dr. Robert A. Warren. Printed and bound in the United States of America. All rights reserved. No part of this book may be reproduced or transmitted in any form or by any means, electronic or mechanical, including photocopying, recording, or by an information storage and retrieval system—except by a reviewer who may quote brief passages in a review to be printed in a magazine or newspaper—without permission in writing from the publisher. For information, please contact Gaynor Publishing, P.O. Box 462, Lightfoot, VA 23090.

Although the author and publisher have made every effort to ensure the accuracy and completeness of information contained in this book, we assume no responsibility for errors, inaccuracies, omissions, or any inconsistency herein. Any slights of people, places, or organizations are unintentional.

First printing 1997

ISBN 0-9652494-0-9

LCCN 96-76825

Editing, design, typesetting, and printing services provided by About Books, Inc., 425 Cedar Street, P.O. Box 1500, Buena Vista, CO 81211, (800) 548-1876.

ATTENTION UNIVERSITIES, COLLEGES, CORPORATIONS, AND PROFESSIONAL ORGANIZATIONS: Quantity discounts are available on bulk purchases of this book for educational purposes or fund raising. Special books or book excerpts can also be created to fit specific needs. For information, please contact Gaynor Publishing, P.O. Box 462, Lightfoot, V0A 23090, (703) 250-4068.

Preface

In 1968, while working on a Master of Science degree in engineering management, I attended a course that dealt with the relationship between the law and the engineering community. During one of the lectures, Morris Shuster, an attorney, invited students to submit an abbreviated resume. I scribbled a few sentences on a piece of paper, and unknowingly began over 25 years of activity as a technical expert for the legal community.

This book is devoted to the interaction between interrogation, which is effective questioning, and testimony, which is effective answering by an expert witness.

Table of Contents

I. Introduction
Overview 1
Interrogation/Testimony 1
Effective Expert Testimony 2
Testimonial Emphasis 2
The Structure of the Book 3

II. Interrogation/Testimony Trends
Overview 5
Societal Considerations in Testimony 6
    Cultural Diversity
    Winning
    Ethics
Technological Considerations in Testimony 9
    Communication Technologies
    Data-Handling Technology
    Diagnostic Technology
Summary 13

III. The Organization as the Foundation for Effective Preparation

Overview 15
Environments 15
Crises 18
Organizations and Adversity 19
Organization Objectives 20
Strategy 20
Corporate and Crisis Management Plans 21
Early Warning System 21
Crisis Management Focal Point 22
Crisis Action Teams 23
  Initial Investigation Team
  Test and Analysis Team
Legal and Public Relations Staffs 26
Outside Experts 27
Communication Central 28
Money and Time 29
Summary 30

IV. Analytical Processes Experts Use

Overview 31
Success 32
Crisis Control 33
Information and Evidence Handling 34
  Organization Information
  Situation-Specific Evidence
Testing 36
  Types of Testing

Test Technique 39
    Site Orientation
    Test Plans and Procedures
    Checklists and Predefined Data Recording Forms
    Video and Still Cameras
    Field Instrumentation
    Laboratory Instrumentation
Analysis 44
    Scientific Theory
    General Practice
    Situation Reality
Analysis Methods and Results 46
    Quantitative Analysis
    Qualitative Analysis
    Analytical Results
    Challenges to Analysis
Reviews 47
Risk Assessment 47
Decision Making 49
Summary 49

V. *Pre-Interrogation Expert Preparations*

Overview 50
Know Objectives, Positions, and Roles 51
    Have or Know the Objective
    Don't Assume Knowledge
    Know the Role
    Know the Reason for Appearing
Gain Command of the Information 56
    Situation Orientation

  Prepared Positions
  Facts and Analyses
  Visual Aids
  Know the Interrogator
 Prebriefs 59
  Mock Interviews
  Murder Boards
  Chit Chat
 Stage Setting 61
 Summary 63

VI. *The Audience, The Interrogator and The Expert Witness*

 Overview 65
 Under Pressure 66
 The Audience 66
  The Neutral Audience
  Friendly Audiences
  Unfriendly Audiences
  Audience Tendencies and Limits
 The Interrogator 70
  The Interrogator Controls the Questions
  The Interrogator Does Not Control the Answers
  Is Not the Audience
 The Expert Witness 72
  The Expert Witness Controls the Answers
  The Expert Witness Does Not Control the Questions
  Influence of the Expert Witness
 Summary 75

VII. Expert Witness Responsibilities

    Overview 77
    Presentation: Answering Questions is Not Enough 77
        Communicator
        Educator
        Image Maker
    The Truth 80
    Credibility 81
    The Result 83
        Consistency
        Persistence
        Success and Winning
    Mistakes 85
    Emotions 86
        Fear
        Humor
        Anger
        Embarrassment
        Concern
    Conflicts of Interest 88
    Counteracting Opposing Arguments 89
    Summary 89

VIII. Interrogators and Their Questions

    Overview 91
    Interrogation Tactics 91
        Theory to Reality
        Hard Ball and Soft Ball
        Slow Down and Speed Up
        Questions as Answers

      Definition Challenges
      Repetition of Similar Questions
      Qualifications versus Knowledge
      "Out-of-Context" Questions
      Emotional Assaults
  Interrogation Games 97
      Threats
      Deception
      Rationalized Fiction
      Deliberate Misquotes and Improper Quotes
      Physical Deprivation
  Questions 100
      "Why" Questions
      "How" Questions
      "What If" Questions
      Bind Questions
      Significant but Irrelevant Questions
      Vague and Thoughtless Questions
  Summary 104

IX. Expert Witnesses and Their Answers

  Overview 105
  Testimonial Tactics 105
      Disclosure Timing
      Maintain Professionalism
      Thoughtful Answers and Acknowledged Limits
      Keep It Simple and Straightforward
      Making a Point

Testimonial Games 109
    Sloppy Preparation
    Acting as Mouthpiece
    Misrepresenting Expertise
    Taking Data for Other Purposes Without Disclosure of Intent
    Introducing Personal Interests into Agreed Position
    "Caving In" or "Selling Out"
Answers 112
    Lack of Knowledge
    No Comment
    Yes andP No
    Change the Subject
    Human Concerns
    Time Pressure
    Take a Break
    Refuse Abuse
    Interview Completion
Code Words and Phrases 115
Summary 116

X. *Final Remarks*

Overview 119
Understanding the Picture Leads to Success 119
The Basis for Success 120
Responsibilities 121
Focus on the Question at Hand 121

Index 123

Introduction

Overview

The interrogation/testimony arena is a stressful place where words and images clash. Attorneys, journalists, politicians, auditors, and interest group advocates use questions as tools to initiate, direct, and control dialogue. Experts must provide answers that address not only the substance of questions but also their motivations and context.

This book addresses the expert's situation and emphasizes approaches and activities needed to improve effectiveness. It recognizes that professional interrogators are increasingly better at what they do, and experts must improve to function within the complex, sophisticated setting that results.

Interrogation/Testimony

Interrogation is questioning designed to achieve a favored outcome in an adversarial dialogue. In a positive sense, an effective interrogation uncovers useful information, stimulates change, and promotes justice. There are valid concerns, however, that modern interrogation practices are counterproductive.

Testimony is the solemn verbal and visual response to adversarial questioning. It is not response under torture or incarceration, although skilled interrogators are often able to apply pressure by creating emotional or physical discomfort. When done in a courtroom, it is legally binding and carries the threat of penalty if perjury is committed.

Testimony often has destructive implications because disagreements between opposing parties are used to expose rather than resolve differences. It is normally associated with a crisis, accident or other singular event.

Effective Expert Testimony

Expert testimony must be highly disciplined, systematic, and survival oriented. It requires that analytical skills, specialized knowledge, pertinent experience, a professional reputation, and organizational authority be employed to authenticate conclusions and opinions. Effective expert testimony depends on truthfulness, thorough preparation, and the ability to present arguments clearly.

Truth is the foundation of the interrogation/testimony dialogue. If it is abused, then the validity and credibility of any argument, regardless of its merit, is destroyed.

Preparation is needed to understand crisis realities, and to identify pitfalls and opportunities. Preparation involves the development of objectives, strategies, and implementation plans that support individual and organization actions. It entails marshaling and controlling the resources needed to succeed in the adversarial environment. It does not, however, ensure a win.

The interrogation/testimony dialogue has a greater meaning than just an exchange of information. Effective expert witnesses take advantage of thorough preparations and truth telling to favorably influence audiences and decisions makers.

Testimonial Emphasis

Much of what will be discussed hereafter is based on the author's experience with attorneys, who are the most educationally prepared interrogators. Many of the examples used will come from the legal environment, although some will come from televised hearings or media interviews so the reader can obtain and use archived information to improve individual preparations and develop expert witness skills.

Emphasis on the legal aspects of interrogation/testimony, however, does not limit the book to the judicial forum. Discussions with journalists, Congressional staff members, auditors, and others indicate interrogation strategies, tactics, and techniques are widely used.

The Structure of the Book

This brief introduction has dealt with the basic definitions of interrogation and testimony. It has introduced truth, thorough preparation, and presentation ability as the foundation for effective expert testimony.

Chapter II will deal with the assumptions and trends that affect the interrogation/testimony environment. Specifically, societal conflict, which focuses on winning, and technological change in communications, data handling, and diagnostics will be addressed.

Chapters III, IV and V will deal with the thorough preparations needed to meet the demands of the adversarial environment. Chapter III will address organization groundwork. Chapter IV will outline an analytical process that supports expert activities. Chapter V will focus on individual preparations.

Chapters VI through IX will deal with the interrogation/testimony dialogue. Chapter VI will address the roles of the interrogator, audience and expert witness. Chapter VII will focus on expert witness responsibilities. Chapters VIII and IX will examine the world of interrogator questions and expert witness answers.

Chapter X concludes the book.

Interrogation/ Testimony Trends

Overview

Societal conflict and technological change dominate contemporary American society.

First, America's institutions are increasingly affected by the demands of a more fragmented, contentious society. The religious, family, and work ethics dominant throughout most of America's history have been, and will continue to be, affected by population and global changes. Experts must be aware of multicultural situations which influence objectivity and professionalism.

Second, America's future depends on its ability to develop, market, and use high-value consumer products, sophisticated industrial equipment, and complicated production and service facilities. Organizations increasingly rely on advances in technology to cut costs, improve quality, meet rapidly changing customer demands, resolve disputes, and remain competitive. In the interrogation/testimony arena, experts use advanced communication, data handling, and diagnostic technologies to understand events, develop and analyze facts, and create arguments and images that educate and influence audiences.

Discussion in this chapter will focus on a general set of assumptions and trends that are a normal and expected part of the expert's environment.

Societal Considerations in Testimony

Societal conflict is having an increasing impact on the resolution of crisis situations because it affects the conduct of adversarial activities and perceptions of success or failure. Arguments are not independent of people, and the way people view right and wrong varies greatly depending on their race, sex, age, ethnic background, and religion.

Cultural Diversity

The most profound changes in the American social structure are the result of continuing cultural diversification. The lack of a shared social foundation causes legislation and adjudication rather than traditional morality and civility to dominate disputes. Government regulations, which implement law, are often the basis for deciding diversity conflicts. Failures and mistakes in the interpretation and use of regulations expose individuals and organizations to investigations and adversarial proceedings. Audits are frequently used as a defense against second guessing in the event something goes wrong.

Cultural diversity directly impacts the expert. Fifty years ago, the legal profession was almost entirely white male. Today, an expert can expect to work for women and minority attorneys, and interrogation disputes often extend beyond case issues. Male/female ploys are common, and it is not unusual for minority lawyers to visibly use their racial or ethnic status to influence a jury. The resulting extracurricular squabbles affect the understanding of problems, professional ethics, and the quality of the interrogation/testimony dialogue.

> *During a deposition, an older male attorney attacked the professional integrity and competency of a younger opposition female attorney. The contemptuous and discourteous comments, which were on the record, became a source of distraction to the expert being deposed. Mistakes and misstatements increased as a result.*

In addition, audiences and juries are also much less uniform. In America's major urban centers, a jury of peers will probably be dominated by minority groups. Language acceptable to a Caucasian Christian male may be offensive to an African-American Muslim female. The English language may not be quickly or universally understood, especially when it is the second language of a jury member.

An appreciation of the importance of cultural diversity can be key to an expert's success.

Winning

In a very fast-paced world governed by proliferating law and media exposé, a win/lose mentality often dominates interrogation/testimony situations. Experts will be pressured to give opinions supporting favored positions and must often deal with discourteous behavior. Intimidation, including outright threats, and misrepresentation of position are used to disrupt thought processes. Quoting out of context is so common the expert should expect it at all times.

> *To create pressure during a deposition, an attorney spent hour after hour shouting and screaming. He used junior attorneys who laughed and snickered, made strange noises, and used derogatory hand gestures to disrupt witnesses. One of the junior attorneys interrupted both nondeposition conversations and bathroom breaks.*

An expert entering the interrogation/testimony arena should realize winning tends to become everything to interrogators and their clients. It constitutes financial survival for irreparably injured individuals, and affects the profits and viability of businesses. Winning can mean budget cuts, layoffs, political firings, and even closure of government and academic institutions. To be effective, an expert must distinguish between the interrogator's responsibility to a client, and the expert's responsibility to the truth.

On a final philosophic note, nearly half a century ago, the term caveat emptor (let the buyer beware) was the prevalent basis for American commercial conduct. Within the past few decades, the situation has almost totally reversed. A business supplying a product is now accountable for the product's design, manufacture, support, use and misuse, and disposal. Products designed and manufactured decades ago often are held to current standards and laws. For example, 1940s electroplating manufacturers regularly used unusual, often toxic compounds in their products. Today, the disposal of that product can involve a multimillion-dollar corporate investment under threat of environmental penalty and criminal prosecution. Neither ownership change, long-term abandonment of use, or claim of ignorance alters the legal requirement for cleanup. Only years of court battles will decide responsibility, and allocation of costs to affected parties.[1] Let the producer and supplier beware!

Ethics

The tremendous pressure to win causes facts and analyses to be skewed by opposing parties. Expert witnesses must guard against being drawn into a web of speculation and advocacy that is unreasonable and potentially damaging to credibility and reputation. Fundamentally, loss of objectivity leads to excessive risk-taking and failure in the interrogation/testimony arena.

> *In a written report, an expert proposed a new solution to a relatively simple problem. Unfortunately, the new solution created greater hazards than those found in the original design. Informal discussions revealed that the expert had been driven to propose this solution by attorney insistence. Attorney bias and expert acceptance undermined the case and led to an unfavorable settlement.*

From both a practical and ethical perspective, it is important for an expert to tell the truth and to represent fully those positions which can be factually and analytically supported and

---

[1] The cost of a judgment may be imposed on the least responsible parties because they have extensive liability insurance coverage.

believed. It is equally important to avoid and refuse to advocate positions which cannot be professionally substantiated.

Experts confronted by media interviewers have a particular problem. Biased reporting is common, and a fair and impartial hearing or outcome cannot be expected. A news interview favoring one side of a controversial matter can, by association, enhance the reputation of an expert who is interviewed. Conversely, an expert having to argue the merits of the opposing point of view is under the microscope of adversity regardless of facts, analysis, and logic.

Whether in courts, politics or the media, prejudiced arguments, muckraking for information, and an emphasis on the correctness of values rather than facts affect the interrogation/testimony dialogue. The harm done to the reputation of an expert, the viability of an organization, or audience understanding is not considered particularly important.

Technological Considerations in Testimony

There is a rapidly growing array of technologies important to the resolution of any adversarial situation. Communication, data handling, and diagnostic technologies help experts clarify situations and educate audiences. Ignorance or misuse of these technologies places an expert at a great disadvantage because the interrogation process involves constant challenges to understanding, conclusion, and opinion.

Communication Technologies

Throughout most of the 19th century, books, magazines, and newspapers connected people around the nation and the world. In the latter half of the 19th century and the early part of the 20th century, however, the telegraph, radio, and telephone provided the basis for an audio communication revolution. Audio technology itself was soon supplanted by motion pictures and television. Today, distinctions between image and fact are clarified or blurred through the use of video and simulation.

Advances in communication technology have a major impact on the interrogation/testimony arena. Interrogators increasingly use video to focus attention. Video leaves little to the imagination because it allows event sequences, timing, and other factual realities to be accurately depicted. It overcomes verbal style and individual charismatic advantages or disadvantages. It is dynamic, exciting, and threatening to opponents. Video is often crucial to success in many criminal proceedings and civil suits because juries are comfortable with the visual formats of television and movies.

Computer simulation is the ultimate in simplifying audience understanding. It can transform almost any data into a realistic visual and graphical mode. Computer simulation can even provide a better representation of events than video recording. Specifically, simulations can highlight selective elements of a problem, and eliminate extraneous and confusing information. Simulations also can be efficiently revised as new facts are introduced or understandings changed. In the future, virtual reality may be able to take anyone to an accident site and help them relive the accident.

The most substantive problems with simulations involve cost of production, representation accuracy, and the potential for bias. To be used in court, simulated images must be able to withstand evidentiary challenges. They must be objective and based on valid data and methodology. They must not be emotionally prejudicial or speculative.

> *In the O.J. Simpson murder case, a number of popular television exposés showed simulated versions of how the dual murders occurred. These simulations, acceptable for television, had no standing in the courts.*

The expert should consider both data gathering and image making during fact finding and testing. Data-gathering activities that do not consider the importance of visual clarity and consistency may be ineffective, costly, and confusing. Furthermore, sole dependence on verbal testimony and simple drawings or photographs may prove inadequate, especially when the situation is complex.

Essentially, an effective expert both testifies and performs. Testifying competency derives from qualifications and rigorous analyses. Performance quality involves appropriate use of language, dress, and presentation techniques.

One additional note: Advances in communication technology will affect instructions for automobiles, airplanes, boats, electronic equipment, and the like. Literacy problems and increasing product complexity undermine the adequacy and effectiveness of written instructions. Warnings, which are a subset of instructions, are often ignored, inadequately understood, or misleading. Visual, as opposed to verbal, warnings may resolve some literacy problems, but they do not provide a comprehensive training experience. Advances in simulations and interactive gaming promise a major training improvement because the impact of customer failings can be incorporated into a game which is both educational and enjoyable.

Data-Handling Technology

The pace of change in data-handling technology has exceeded that of communication technology. As late as the 1960s, the engineer commonly used a slide rule. The calculator was an expensive, complicated luxury. The transistor and integrated circuit were just beginning to emerge from the laboratory. The computer was a massive and expensive computation tool available only to major government agencies, large corporations, and scientific institutions.

Today, data-handling technologies pervade every element of American society. Computer giants such as Apple, IBM, and Microsoft continuously bring an extraordinary array of useful facts and data manipulation tools to homes, businesses, educational institutions, and society at large. Computer-integrated design and specialized data bases support technical analyses. Artificial intelligence provides interactive "expertise in a box." Computer-based networks increasingly are used to improve organization efficiency and effectiveness because such networks allow concurrent use of data by teams of specialists. In the near future, advances in the information infrastructure will permit the assemblage of world class "virtual" expert teams and enterprises.

The expert is required to absorb and understand sophisticated and voluminous amounts of written and visual data, and to sort all of the facts and allegations into a reasonable set of conclusions and opinions. Expert teams are often needed to integrate scientific and technical findings because specialists who develop and understand a particular data set may not have interdisciplinary knowledge and experience. Data overload[2] can occur when opposing parties in a lawsuit organize data in ways that substantiate different positions.

It is apparent that computer competency, especially in the manipulation of data leading to graphics and simulations, is required of the expert or, more likely, someone on an expert team.

Diagnostic Technology

The data-handling and communication technology revolutions are obvious to the world. Major corporations, as well as government agencies, are aggressively competing to inform the world. There is, however, a subtle revolution in diagnostics that substantially underpins the communication and data-handling revolutions.

Progress in miniaturization allows diagnostic mechanisms and sensors to be embedded into products and process streams. Increasingly smart or even brilliant devices are capable of controlling automated facilities and insuring that equipment is operating efficiently. Many of these devices are linked to instruments that record the extensive amounts of data needed to regulate product performance or industrial activity. When an accident occurs, a record probably exists either from onsite or remote readout devices. Such records have powerful evidentiary and analytical implications.

---

[2] The volume of information associated with lawsuits has grown extensively over the past 25 years. In the early 1970s, police and witness statements were often the common basis for expert analysis and subsequent written reports. Today, depositions, videos, and special studies even for small cases fill file drawers. Preparation for deposition or trial represents thousands of dollars and many hours of review.

Miniaturization has led to a radical improvement in the measurement and test equipment used by experts. In the past, inspection, fact-finding testing and accident reconstruction activities were largely dependent on simple, rugged mechanical devices such as the tape measure and carpenter's level. Sophisticated diagnostic equipment was almost exclusively found in laboratories.

In the 1980s, reliable electronic field test instruments became available. The data gathered using electronic instruments is more accurate and precise than provided by most mechanical devices. Furthermore, test results can be processed more rapidly when test instruments are directly linked to computers. Near real-time data-handling capability can be important during testing because it may allow for quick adaptation to newly discovered situations.

The precision and diagnostic diversity of current laboratory instrumentation is even more spectacular than field instruments. Laboratory instrumentation is regularly used to obtain data at micro-structural, molecular and atomic levels. (A single human hair, for example, provides more than enough material for genetic testing or electron microscopy matching.) Laboratory devices allow for the elimination of extraneous environmental effects. Laboratory investigation is an invaluable adjunct to field testing, especially in situations where the field conditions are poor and testing is difficult to control.

While it is important that experts be good data diagnosticians, some cautions are appropriate. Many experts have a tendency to over emphasize data taking to ensure sufficiency; this is costly and can lead to confusion in sorting, understanding, and using facts. Excessive focus on data-taking precision can lead to a substitution of analytical elegance for situation objectives, and may indicate the initial purpose of testing was not fully understood. In the world of the expert, "Better is the enemy of good enough."

Summary

The impact of sociology and technology on the interrogation/testimony arena has been outlined in this chapter. Among the important concerns to the expert is the impact of cultural diversity on logic and reasonableness. Insensitive or prejudiced dialogue can divert juries and audiences from sound arguments. There is also little doubt communication, data-handling and diagnostic technologies are important because of their power to create bias, clarify truth, or compensate for communication inadequacies.

Fundamentally, experts are ethically bound to do their best to insure that a truthful representation of reality is effectively presented to the audience. An expert who understands the societal situation and takes advantage of the opportunities created by technology can develop a clear understanding of the facts, perform superior analyses, and respond better to interrogation/testimony demands. Improved expert effectiveness contributes to success, but it cannot guarantee a win.

In the next few chapters, discussions will focus on support for the expert. A disciplined analysis process resulting in a risk assessment will be used to bridge organizational activities and individual preparations.

The Organization as the Foundation for Effective Preparations

Overview

Effective response to a crisis requires an organization's resources and personnel be marshaled in a systematic, disciplined, and survival-oriented manner. Crisis objectives and strategies must be established and related to overall business objectives. A crisis management plan and early warning system should be developed and implemented. A crisis management focal point should be established to provide a stable base of operations. Ad hoc crisis action teams that ensure the availability of information and evidence, plan for and conduct tests, and communicate the organization's position will be needed. Investment and scheduling decisions must also be made.

Discussion in this chapter will focus on the organization as the foundation to prepare for and counteract adverse situations.

Environments

Judicial, legislative, regulative, media, and interest group environments have distinctive characteristics. It is the responsibility of an organization involved in a crisis to recognize the implications of each of these environments and to prepare individual experts accordingly.

In the American judicial system, confrontation by examination is deliberate, and attorneys spend years learning and practicing the interrogation trade. Trials, which are the culmination of many judicial efforts, are governed by a formal legal structure and a reasonably well-defined set of rules. Plaintiffs and defendants are allowed to argue the merits of opposing claims before a jury of their peers (if desired), and a presiding judge is expected to maintain decorum and fairness in the courtroom. Discovery of relevant facts and opinions takes place prior to trial. Depositions, which are part of the discovery process, are unencumbered by the presence of a judge. And attorneys frequently mix facts, images, and emotional assaults to test witnesses. Of importance, the judicial environment is fragmented by cultural and regional conflicts transcending specific case issues. A just result cannot be guaranteed.

> *In one civil action, the plaintiff attorney, members of the local police force, and the family and friends of the deceased were from the same ethnic community. After local jury selection, the defense, which was from out of town agreed to settle the case for $500,000. A review of discovery information indicated the accident was the fault of the deceased; however, an adverse jury verdict, likely under the circumstances, would have led to corporate bankruptcy.*

Congress and most other legislative bodies are ruled by political expediency, predefined rules of order, and the appearance of professional courtesy. Legislators, who are constantly running for reelection, help constituents with problems, support their districts through committee activities, and sponsor and shepherd legislation. Legislative hearings often follow a particular administrative format. A committee chairperson allows witnesses to make introductory statements that are topically relevant and emphasize significant issues and positions. Legislators then question witnesses to better understand facts and opinions and to posture for political purposes. Question time is closely controlled by the committee chairperson; however, question content, as long as it is germane to the topic at hand, is left to the discretion of individual legislators. Because many hearings are now televised, image making and sensationalized arguments that attract the attention of the media and the electorate increasingly dominate substance in legislative forums.

The media environment is without a real, enforceable standard of conduct. Reporters are ruthless in pursuit of a story and can seldom be controlled by circumstance, reason, or appeal. Competitive pressures often lead to partial or mangled versions of the truth. The news media has also extended journalistic interrogation beyond reporting. Infotainment and investigative exposés blur the distinction between reality and fantasy.

Audits and investigations occur as a result of demands to ensure compliance with law and regulation. Explicit instructions govern the rights and responsibilities of the auditors, investigators and individuals being examined. If, however, corporate personnel do not ask about these instructions then almost any audit or investigation can extend beyond a determination of the facts and into issues of right and wrong. The result is increased organization and individual exposure to blame.

Special interest group meetings are probably best viewed as emotional events. Images dominate interest group forums because the agenda, alternatives, and answers generally are known before the questions are asked. Interest group representatives almost certainly have command of the pros and cons of their narrowly defined positions and often are effective interrogators even though they lack formal interrogation skills.[3] In meetings involving opposing interest groups, shouting matches where noise and passion equate to affirmation of position are increasingly used to resolve issues. Civil disturbances and disobedience of the law are not unusual.

It is essential that organizational objectives, strategic planning, and crisis management actions take into account the nature of these environments. All too often, an individual being interrogated as a corporate representative makes erroneous assumptions

---

[3] Attorneys often represent interest groups. The expanding body of law designed to balance competing interests is complex and contains civil and criminal penalties. Pro-choice and pro-life activism, for example, has been the subject of decades of legislation and numerous judicial decisions.

about the context of his or her remarks. It is probable that ignorance of the adversarial environment will undermine the organization's position and the individual's credibility and effectiveness. It can also be costly.

> *In dealing with Congress, one federally regulated industry found it useful to accept blame. Politicians had the opportunity to criticize the industry and to appear aggressive in defense of constituent interests. These admissions, however, were also used by plaintiff attorneys during civil litigation to prove industry malfeasance. Literally millions of dollars were lost as a result.*

Crises

A crisis is an emergency that temporarily destabilizes normal activity within an organization. It is obvious that the Exxon *Valdez* oil spill, the Union Carbide Bhopal pesticide plant disaster, and the New York World Trade Center bombing were crises because of the suddenness and magnitude of the problems they represented. The organizations involved were immediately compelled to control, investigate, and resolve these crises to achieve stability and to reduce the intense scrutiny and social pressures they engendered.

There are creeping crises, however, that begin with little substance but explode into major concerns for the organizations involved. A congressional hearing that focuses on dissent and controversy becomes a nightmare for agency executives because they are sent scrambling to defend even the best decisions under threat of sanction. A media exposé suggests that there is a problem meeting a federal regulation, and a stockholder revolt or corporate takeover becomes a real possibility. A school bus accident that is the fault of the driver and inadequate equipment maintenance evolves into a multimillion dollar judgment against the bus manufacturer.

There are perceived crises that have little substance but refuse to disappear because of images and emotions. Nuclear power plants are publicly perceived to be time bombs waiting to go off even though their long-term safety records are superior to those of most other commercial enterprises. Such perceived crises become part of day-to-day business operations because they are perpetual in nature.

This book generally addresses the event that suddenly assumes crisis proportions, requiring organization and individual attention outside the normal course of constructive business.

Organizations and Adversity

Senior executives, managers, and workers normally operate in a cooperative and constructive manner in most business situations. Therefore, most employees are not naturally adept at dealing with the destructive criticism found in the interrogation/testimony arena.

> *Many of presidential candidate Ross Perot's 1992 interviews with the media are classic in making this distinction. He continuously tried to be cooperative and civil while the reporters covering his campaign obviously sought the one sensational blunder or controversial statement that would make national headlines. To combat media filtering, Perot purchased television time for infomercials.*

Organization procedures and administrative structures must be in place prior to the onset of a crisis so that individuals can be effectively prepared. Rushed preparations and inadequate coordination virtually ensure that crisis information and images will be misunderstood and mishandled. Under such circumstances, progress toward meeting objectives and achieving success will be less than satisfactory. Human interactions will become contentious as people question each other's knowledge, experience, mental stability, and commitment. (All too often, senior corporate officials participate in crisis planning activities as an afterthought and do not interact with other corporate personnel in a timely fashion.)

Adversarial activities are not the constructive criticism of a valued customer. While good can come from criminal and civil actions, media exposés and investigations, the underlying intent is hostile. Winning and losing are inherent in the interrogation/testimony arena.

Organization Objectives

The basic objectives of organizations are related to their intended place in American society. Private corporations exist to make a profit by providing a product or service. Academic institutions exist to educate students and to perform and publish research. Governmental agencies exist to enforce laws and regulate associated activity.

In crisis management, the primary objectives of the organization are temporarily subordinated as preservation of assets and defense of organization reputation and stability become the objectives. Damage control, taking the organization's case public, and combating unfairness are all examples of crisis objectives important to an organization. They are not, however, comfortable objectives and do not often enhance corporate effectiveness.

A crisis will consume organization resources, disrupt efficient operations, and possibly threaten survival. The organization must have crisis objectives that provide the focus for risk assessment activities, allow clear and easy understanding by individuals, and tie to the more basic and productive organization purposes. The chance for a successful crisis outcome is increased using this approach.

Strategy

An organization needs a clear and compelling institutional strategy that supports crisis objectives. A crisis objective to limit damage, for example, may lead to a defensive strategy where the information disclosed is limited to the facts. A crisis objective to preserve reputation may suggest an open strategy which involves acceptance of blame and a willingness to make things right as a responsible corporate citizen. A crisis objective to combat unfairness may require a vocal and aggressive protest strategy and involve the use of organization resources in a litigation or advertising campaign.

Corporate and Crisis Management Plans

Organizations, of course, develop and maintain a variety of business plans which reflect institutional objectives, interests and problems, and articulate concern for current and future customer needs. Many business plans, however, do not fully represent the institutional situation. In the interrogation/testimony arena, such plans can confuse or create an impression of deception, lack of control, and irresponsibility. It is more than conceivable that courtroom drama will expose inadequate planning as a precursor to thoughtlessness in product design, manufacture, and use.

Crisis plans evolve from crisis objectives and strategies, but they must ultimately be integrated with business plans so that resources are used wisely.

Both the business and crisis management plans should be sufficiently understandable that key corporate personnel can explain their relationship to a crisis. Good plans support individual preparations and minimize the emotional stresses and pressures of a crisis. They give the organization an improved opportunity to survive a crisis with reputation and stability intact.[4]

Early Warning System

The unique problems of an unexpected crisis are easily recognized when the organization is caught up in its ongoing whirlwind. Decisions that affect the future viability of the organization are often forced and are not thoroughly deliberated. The crisis consumes corporate resources at an explosive rate. Individual employees are forced to react to a continuous stream of annoying and frustrating external demands and to act spontaneously to counter the negative publicity that destroys hard-earned good will.

---

[4] The National Association of Manufacturers has published a guide entitled *Crisis! Crisis!*, which helps managers to be proactive in dealing with crises. It is practical and realistic.

Many crises, however, can be readily anticipated even though their magnitude and time of occurrence cannot be predicted. A fire at a petroleum plant is not unexpected even if a high level of safety is designed in and continuously maintained. Theft of research and development secrets from a defense laboratory is not unanticipated regardless of security and the prospects of criminal sanction. An earthquake in southern California is likely to disrupt the functioning of a highway.

Crisis anticipation activities depend on the development of criteria that trigger an early warning system. For example, maintenance delays, loss of trained technicians, failure of a safety inspection, fire and explosion in a competitor's plant, and a whistle blower complaint could be criteria that trigger the organization's early warning system.

Crisis anticipation activities also involve the creation of most probable crisis scenarios. Organization personnel can then game and practice solutions.

An early warning system that ties crisis objectives, strategies, and plans to current operations should be developed. The organization will thus become more proactive when dealing with the ambiguities and confusion of a crisis.

Crisis Management Focal Point

The corporation should have someone preassigned to crisis management. This individual, the crisis management focal point, should be immediately notified in the event of an emergency and should lead the initial response activities.

The crisis management focal point must be prepared and empowered to act quickly and efficiently to help the organization and its personnel make the transition from normalcy to crisis (and back). He or she should have direct access to the highest corporate decision levels. The crisis management focal point can have normal line responsibilities within the organization, but must be relieved of such responsibilities if the magnitude of the crisis threatens organization stability and survival. It is important for the corporation to select an individual who is able to be dispassionate and objective under pressure, is extremely knowledgeable about corporate operations and information, and is an effective communicator.

The crisis management focal point works with corporate executives to establish crisis objectives and strategies and to obtain the personnel and resources needed to deal with crisis risks. He or she develops and maintains the organization's early warning system, establishes expert witness training programs for corporate personnel, and creates a detailed crisis plan which assigns crisis action responsibilities to corporate divisions and individuals. The crisis management focal point helps make crisis response part of institutional business practice rather than an uncontrolled imposition.

The University of Wisconsin-Madison's Department of Engineering provides numerous professional development courses that address product liability and expert-witness training. Most courses are heavily attended by high-level corporate executives who have specific crisis management responsibilities. These courses also act as a clearinghouse where expert consultants can interact in a benign setting with potential customers and adversaries.

Crisis Action Teams

The crisis management focal point needs to be supported by crisis action teams. These teams vary in composition over time and often contain technical specialists brought in from the outside. Crisis action teams exist for limited periods of time and are focused on the details of a crisis and related objectives rather than the normal course of business.[5]

Initial Investigation Team

An initial investigation team consisting of key technical, legal, and public affairs experts should be used to assemble facts and relevant information on short notice. To minimize confusion

---

[5] Flexible and agile organizations can be readily customized to meet crisis requirements. Organization employees have an intimate understanding of their products and services and represent a powerful knowledge and experience baseline.

in responding to a crisis, team membership should be predefined so that the crisis management focal point can quickly assemble the human resources needed to handle rapidly changing workload demands.

The initial investigation team should collect and organize evidence and information, perform a rough, first-cut situation assessment, draft initial definitions of crisis objectives and strategies, identify gaps in information and the chain of logic, and outline alternative theories of what happened. Team members should provide direct and honest advice to the corporate decision-makers and help with rumor control. It is important to insulate the members of the initial investigation team from the demands of interrogators. At the early stages of a crisis, publicly exposed positions and ideas become the baseline for future discussion and decisions. Questions and answers should be funneled through the crisis management focal point to ensure consistency with current factual understandings and organization positions.

Members of the initial investigation team should be educated in information- and evidence-handling techniques. Knowing how to locate and use relevant information, perform site inspections and preserve evidence, and organize information and evidence to facilitate analyses is crucial to effectiveness in future interrogation/testimony activities.

One final note: The initial investigation team is going to be strongly affected by the turbulence of the crisis. Nevertheless, team members must remain dispassionate and maintain a strong commitment to objectively understand the causes and impact of a crisis. Emotional tirades or assignment of blame are not productive because they cloud judgment and undermine efforts to achieve an effective initial risk assessment. The crisis management focal point should have the power to build and maintain the investigative team and to add or remove individuals on short notice. (Overwrought individuals do not think clearly and may become physically and mentally ill.)

During the initial buildup for the Vietnam War, the Commander of the Philadelphia Naval Shipyard ordered all civilian employees to work minimum 10-hour days, six days per week. He also eliminated vacations. After six months of intense activity, the Commander was forced to cancel the order because supervisors reported that increased worker illness and distress were adversely affecting productivity.

Test and Analysis Team

The initial investigative team needed to control the crisis will likely be replaced by a long-term test and analysis team whose members are better suited to solving specific problems. Because crucial aspects of crises or urgent situations cannot always be immediately diagnosed, the test and analysis team must work to verify initial investigative findings, sort out conflicts in information and evidence, perform field and laboratory tests, analyze and clarify crisis explanations, and develop presentations. Test and analysis team activities focus on meeting crisis management objectives and producing a risk assessment for use in corporate decision-making.

The test and analysis team should be led by an individual who looks at the crisis from a comprehensive and systematic perspective and works closely with the crisis management focal point. The team leader should be supported by relevant technical experts, analysts skilled in statistics and the use of risk management and trade-off study techniques, and audiovisual designers who can develop graphics, videos and computer-aided depictions of crisis sequences. Accurately engineered images based on first-class, realistic testing and analysis are powerful persuasion tools in the adversarial environment.

A team of experts consisted of a material engineer, fire and explosion and marine systems consultants, an instrumentation specialist, and a camera crew. This team easily cost thousands of dollars per day.

It is probable that membership on the initial investigation and test and analysis teams will overlap. This is beneficial if a documented, traceable process was used to preserve and protect initial crisis information and evidence. Team overlap may prove controversial if the initial investigation team members removed evidence from the incident site before it was catalogued or properly examined because this disrupts the chain of evidence. Unfortunately, the rush to get answers often causes mistakes that abuse recognized evidence and ignore or damage unrecognized evidence.

Members of the test and analysis team must guard against individual prejudices and preconceived notions that bias data gathering and testing. Analysis efforts can be debased if improper procedures are used. Further bias, if discovered, may be treated as dishonesty. When possible, the test and analysis team leader should not be the individual most centrally affected by the crisis outcome because a conflict of interest can arise or be alleged by opponents.

Legal and Public Relations Staffs

Many corporations vest crisis management with the legal staff. While this makes sense if there are concerns about litigation, it strongly focuses organization activities on legal defense rather than the overall demands of the crisis. Lawyers are trained in the law and, therefore, concentrate on exposure to lawsuits or criminal proceedings. They normally are not specialists in product or process technology.

If the corporation or agency has a public relations office, then it should be used. People in this office are expected to support the corporate image and reputation in dealing with the media and interest groups. They should also know how to protect the organization against unwelcome and unauthorized interrogation activities. During a crisis, the public relations office should assist the crisis management focal point in setting up and managing communications with journalists, investigators, and officials.

The legal and public relations staffs are necessary and invaluable to an effective crisis response. As such, they should be included in the creation and development of the crisis management structure of the organization as well as on the crisis action teams.

Outside Experts

It is important for institutions unfamiliar with the handling and management of interrogation/testimony interactions to employ organizations who know how to function effectively in adversarial environments. Many law firms focus on the legal specialties needed to handle one type of crisis. There are other firms that provide useful communication and technical specialties:

> *Rowan and Blewitt Incorporated of Washington, DC, is a crisis and media management organization. ATA Associates of Houston, Texas is a forensic engineering and investigation organization that also maintains an extensive graphics and animation capability. The Technical Advisory Service for Attorneys (TASA) of Fort Washington, Pennsylvania is an expert referral service with nearly 25,000 experts and over 5,500 categories of expertise.*

Outside experts often are added to the organization's crisis management team because they provide a capability that is needed but not resident in the organization. Outside experts are usually more objective than organization employees. They are useful in controlling employee emotions, ensuring that risks are appropriately weighed, and presenting positions in a reasonable manner.

Outside experts, however, can find themselves in conflict with organization employees because their dissection of an organization's product or process can be disquieting and embarrassing. To improve team cohesion, an organization should not wait an extended period of time before employing an outside expert. The passage of time will cause information and evidence to be lost or degraded, will firmly establish the organization's theory of how the crisis happened, and can substantially increase expense because the expert must redo or undo prior analyses.

> *A processing facility regularly used a caustic chemical for refrigeration. An accident occurred when a flexible hose used to transport the chemical broke and spewed caustic material into a worker's eyes. The initial accident theory, accepted by both the facility and the hose manufacturer representatives, was that the hose material was defective. An examination by an outside expert revealed the hose could have broken only as a result of a procedural mistake by the worker. The hose manufacturer, however, had already paid $250,000 to the worker.*

Communication Central

The first communication site will probably be the crisis location. The urgency of the situation, the needs of firefighters, police or others, and the aggressive actions of reporters may make factually accurate discussion difficult and encourage unwarranted speculation. The organization must find temporary quarters, even a plot of grass behind a shed, where quiet, confidential conversations can take place.

As the crisis evolves, a more formal centralized communication facility will be needed. To be conducive to effective dialogue, communication facilities should have appropriate lighting, comfortable tables and chairs, sound and video systems, telephones and facsimile machines, computers, and copiers.[6] Communication facilities should be comfortable to reduce stress. In small-to medium-sized organizations, special communication facilities may not exist. A conference room can be used, but the disruption of normal business by groups of outsiders may be traumatic. Consideration should be given to using temporary shelters or rented space nearby.

The communication situation may permit multiple corporate representatives and experts to answer questions in a panel format. Questions can then be answered by the most knowledge-

---

[6] The previously referenced National Association of Manufacturers crisis management manual has a number of checklists that help with communication preparation.

able person while others on the panel have time to think. Caution must be exercised because a public disagreement about the crisis by members of the corporate team is substantial grist for subsequent interrogations. There should be one and only one panel spokesperson directing communication traffic.

Of importance, communication and analysis activity should be separated. Analysis is a systematic activity that requires concentration and thought. It is difficult to do effective analysis while being distracted and interrupted by conversations that are potentially relevant to analysis outcomes. Furthermore, analytical theorizing and speculations not intended for public consumption may be inadvertently disclosed.

Money and Time

When a crisis hits, the organization is thrown off balance and placed in a reactive mode. Under these circumstances, the organization will spend money and use its people and facilities as needed. While crisis containment is possible over time, investment and schedule control is difficult in the near term.

It is extremely important, however, to make long-term investment decisions as soon as possible. Unplanned catch up investments lead to unpleasant surprises, loss of important information, confusion between internal and outside experts, an inadequate risk assessment, and missed opportunities to resolve the situation. Lack of investment planning also means that crisis action teams may persist far beyond their useful life and consume resources better employed in productive ventures. Experts, under unplanned circumstances, may overuse technology and take excessive amounts of data. Attorneys may take unnecessary depositions. Graphic artists may create overly sophisticated graphics and simulations. There should be no blank check under the presumption that large amounts of money and activity will guarantee a win.

In one memorable civil suit, nearly half a million dollars was spent on behalf of a partially blind drunk plaintiff who hit a parked car while speeding without lights at night. The money was spent in the hope that more investment, regardless of acknowledged risk, would somehow translate into a win.

Summary

This chapter outlined the importance of setting objectives, selecting strategies, planning, and using organization resources to promote an effective response to the demands of a crisis. It provided general guidance for mobilizing the organization and strongly recommended an early warning system and crisis management focal point be established. It focused on the development of crisis action teams to improve information gathering, evidence preservation, test planning and conduct, and analysis and risk assessment activities.

In the next chapter, discussion will focus on the use of analytical processes that tie the organization to individual interrogation/testimony preparations.

Analytical Processes Experts Use

Overview

Analysis makes crisis knowledge understandable and useful for organizations and individuals.

The analytical process begins with efforts to control the immediate crisis. Although crisis resolution is paramount at this juncture, consideration should be given to preserving damaged products or facilities so function can be restored and explanations developed.

Information and evidence should be carefully collected, organized, and evaluated so the analysis will be logical and defensible. Subsequent testing, which adds information to clarify what is known or suspected and to fill in factual gaps, should be done as appropriate. Analytical definitions, boundaries and methods should be intelligently selected, and then verified as appropriate for the situation. Analysis results and associated risk assessments which underpin decision making should be unambiguous, even though probabilistic in nature.

Discussion in this chapter will focus on an analytical process that clarifies crisis theories and positions, supports or undermines the credibility of conclusions and opinions, and helps educate and influence audiences.

Success

A successful crisis outcome is defined in terms of corporate objectives. Success may be freedom from civil liability and criminal prosecution or national recognition of perseverance under extreme circumstances. Success, as in the case of the Exxon *Valdez*, may be the loss of billions of dollars but the preservation of Exxon's corporate reputation as a responsible national and world citizen. Success does not mean win. It means doing the best possible under the circumstances.

Success, which may ultimately sustain organization and individual survival, emerges from coordination and commitment. Action teams operating in a purposeful manner buoy confidence and support interrogation/testimony activities. Plans for using funds, facilities, and equipment in a cost-effective, controlled manner demonstrate foresight.

Success is based on the use of a disciplined analytical process which efficiently and effectively handles information and evidence from the crisis and subsequent testing. Measurement criteria and verified methodologies that provide relevant results and address alternatives and sensitivity to change are crucial.

Success requires systematic thinking. New ideas, changes, and surprises are to be expected, and careful construction of each step in the analytical process is needed to ensure the results are as accurate as possible at all times. An objective review of analysis findings at key junctures is important to ensure that everyone involved is on the same sheet of music. Figure 1 diagrams the analytical process flow that will be discussed hereafter.

Crisis Control

An old adage says, "An ounce of prevention is worth a pound of cure." Many institutions use human factors and safety engineering disciplines, safety training, special equipment and facilities, and a substantial number of resources to prevent crises. Human beings, however, along with their products and processes are not perfect and crisis control is needed.

Analytical Processes Experts Use

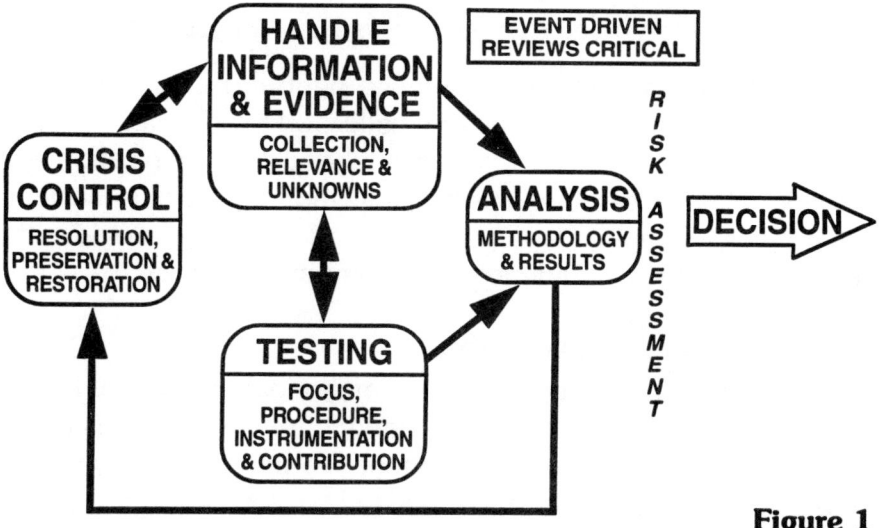

Figure 1

In a crisis, the organization's crisis management preparations are put to use. This involves not only immediate crisis *resolution*, but *preservation* of information and evidence, and concern for *restoration* of function for testing and subsequent return to use.

Preservation of evidence increases the probability that crisis analyses will be based on facts. Careful preservation may lead directly to cause. It may also help to infer cause when evidence is missing.

> *In a boating case, a fire and explosion expert was able to use accident photographs to localize the fire source to a space which contained a forgotten temporary repair of a fuel line. During the trial, it was successfully inferred that the temporary repair was the most probable source of a fuel leak, and therefore, the cause of the accident.*

Restoration supports causality investigations and allows testing to be performed on the accident item rather than an exemplar. Careless handling of post-crisis items, however, undermines restoration and creates hazards in subsequent testing and use.

Information and Evidence Handling

Data is presumed to be value neutral. Its adequacy and accuracy depends on source and collection procedures. To have value, data must be studied and analyzed for organization and individual purposes. Organization information, which is available as a result of day-to-day operations and practices, provides the context for a crisis. Evidence is the remains of a crisis.

Organization Information

Institutionally available information which arrives from a wide variety of dependable and undependable sources is essential to success in crisis management. To be useful, however, it must be related to crisis objectives and contribute to an explanation of crisis events.

Organization information usually provides clues to understanding. In many instances, designs have been prototyped or production tested in small numbers. Management information systems often contain urgently needed information. Information assembled from diverse sources, however, will have to be specially controlled. Properly managed information contributes to long-term analysis and risk assessment success!

Information gathered from improperly maintained files and archives can be a problem. Interrogators disrupt arguments by noting information inadequacies and conflicts. Incomplete or missing information disrupts attempts to reconstruct the history of a product or process. Information gaps are costly because additional resources are needed to search for or recreate data. While damaged and incomplete evidence is to be expected in emergency situations, inadequate, incomplete, and conflicting organization information damages credibility and reputation because it gives the appearance of sloppiness or lack of attention to detail.

Relevant information is also found outside the organization. Many industries have standards and practices which constitute a common body of knowledge to be applied to design, manufacture, support, and operation of products and processes. Industry standards are crucial to the interrogation/testimony situation because they are the baseline for comparing what is with what should be. Violations of industry and government standards and practices are serious indicators of malpractice or malfeasance. (Industry standards are found in technical libraries and are increasingly available on computer disks or networks.)

Situation-Specific Evidence

Evidence is the most precious commodity in the expert's world. While the organizational information gathered is generally relevant, evidence is the indicator of crisis realities.

To preserve evidence, initial investigations should be well organized, careful fact-finding exercises. Well-designed interviews often uncover key evidentiary issues and support discovery of the unusual.

Evidence quality and quantity are crucial to the credibility of arguments, and missing, abused or damaged pieces of evidence are certain to cause disputes. It is imperative, therefore, that evidence be managed and used only under controlled and documented conditions. If evidence must be altered or destroyed, an understanding of the intended result and a thorough appreciation for test methodology and the limits of testing must be clearly articulated. Extraordinary care is mandated because much potential evidence is destroyed by the incident itself, by individuals responding to the crisis situation, by unknowledgeable investigators or injured parties, by the effects of time and environment, or by reconstruction efforts.

Experts use evidence to develop primary and alternate theories of the cause of a crisis. Different theories evolve based on evidence conflicts and the variations they engender. Notably, even virtual certainty of theory correctness leaves room for debate and mistake.

A manufacturer was blamed for a steering deficiency that was assumed to be the cause of a boating accident. The initial theory of the accident was the boat operator lost control of his boat because of the inherent rapid response characteristics associated with the stick steering design. During deposition, the operator outlined a different accident scenario. He said the stick was not initially responsive when moved and then suddenly and unpredictably turned the boat. This suggested a problem internal to the steering mechanism. Subsequent investigation revealed broken gear teeth and a number of applications of different greases - indicating owner rather than factory-authorized work had been done. The character of the lawsuit was changed by this discovery.

Experts should use evidence to understand investigative needs and limitations. They should not use it to focus the investigation on preferred outcomes. Prejudicial thinking is dangerous in the adversarial environment because relevant evidence and subsequent risks may be ignored or misunderstood. It is a common tendency in civil suits for opposing sides to focus on a single explanation of an incident. The effective expert suspends judgment of right or wrong and focuses on what is probable or improbable.

Testing

Test activity begins with an examination of the situation, and an assessment of the potential worth of future investigative, fact-finding and accident reconstruction efforts. Testing is used to resolve theoretical and practical ambiguities associated with a crisis by filling evidentiary and information gaps. It helps overcome the limitations of initial crisis response efforts. Eventually, test and evaluation results become a critical part of analysis and, therefore, support effective risk assessments and decision making.[7]

---

[7] A requirements analysis should be done prior to testing to ensure that sufficient data of reasonable accuracy and precision will be obtained and that extraneous and, therefore, costly and potentially confusing data will not be taken. Test plans, approaches, and instrumentation needs should also be carefully deliberated.

Types of Testing

Inspections are used to confirm physical properties. They are utilized to verify that a reconstructed or exemplar system accurately represents the appropriate crisis configuration and can, therefore be used as a valid basis for fact finding or reconstruction testing and subsequent analysis. Inspection involves taking pertinent dimensions or material samples, recording relevant site and situation details, and cataloging configuration changes and differences that may influence comparability arguments.

During an inspection prior to fact-finding testing, it was discovered that the accident might have involved a different outboard motor configuration than was mounted on the boat. Since motor configuration was relevant to the accident, a number of different sets of test data had to be taken. Testing, which was originally scheduled for half a day, ultimately took two days.

Fact-finding testing to obtain a scientific or engineering explanation for an incident is not to be confused with inspection or reconstruction testing. Fact-finding testing, unlike inspection, is functionally dynamic. It is done to understand how scientific or engineering principles apply to an accident and to evolve relevant performance curves. To do effective fact-finding testing, it is important to measure critical performance parameters (such as speed) at settings that bracket the accident situation. All viable incident scenarios should be examined so the resulting data can support the analysis of alternatives. Fact-finding testing is costly because it often involves extensive repetition to ensure data set accuracy and completeness. It is important to minimize data-taking activities that are not useful in explaining the incident because such activity may become a source of confusion and contention.

To obtain a complete performance envelope, an expert ran numerous tests well outside the range of accident conditions. The expert had to explain why such data were taken even though there was clearly no relevance to accident is-

sues. Opposition attorneys claimed this was a fishing expedition caused by a lack of adequate evidence to support plaintiff claims.

Reconstructive testing is intended to provide a single explanation of an accident. Such testing requires substantial knowledge of the actual incident, possibly from a videotape, and close control of test sequences, conditions, and assumptions. Variation must be kept to a minimum or, if possible, eliminated from testing. Reconstructive testing is highly configuration dependent and must conform to the accident environment. Lack of precision, system configuration control, or environmental conformance makes reconstructive testing suspect and potentially inadmissible in court.

Fact-finding and reconstructive testing can be dangerous. Accidents are uncontrolled events that occur in seconds. They involve rapid and unpredictably chaotic effects. Accidents do occur during fact-finding and reconstructive testing when the boundaries of normal operations are exceeded. Notably, fact-finding or reconstructive testing is often performed on restored equipment or facilities. While restoration may recreate the functions needed to define accident theories and give the appearance of form, it often leaves some of the degrading effects of accident damage or improper preservation.

The testing of a high-performance bass boat involved a number of high-speed turns. In one of the turns, the operator's seat pulled loose from the floor and dumped the operator on his back. Fortunately, a kill switch cut the power to the boat and prevented an ejection or uncontrolled rogue run across a small lake.

The relationships between inspection, fact-finding testing, and reconstructive testing is shown in Figure 2, which follows.

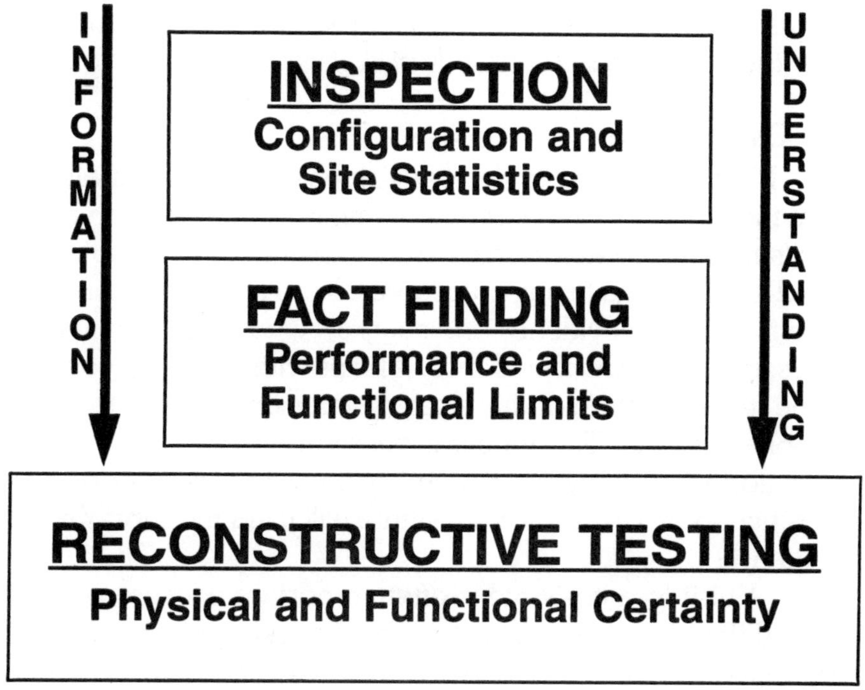

Analytical Processes Experts Use

```
I                                    U
N    ┌─────────────────────────┐     N
F    │      INSPECTION         │     D
O    │   Configuration and     │     E
R    │    Site Statistics      │     R
M    └─────────────────────────┘     S
A                                    T
T    ┌─────────────────────────┐     A
I    │     FACT FINDING        │     N
O    │    Performance and      │     D
N    │   Functional Limits     │     I
│    └─────────────────────────┘     N
▼                                    ▼G
┌──────────────────────────────────────┐
│      RECONSTRUCTIVE TESTING          │
│   Physical and Functional Certainty  │
└──────────────────────────────────────┘
```

Figure 2

Test Technique

There is no substitute for the recognition and control of relevant variables during inspection, fact-finding testing, and event reconstruction. The smallest flaw in technique will be magnified by interrogation/testimony hostilities.

During the William Kennedy Smith rape trial, the defense used the results of investigative testing to prove the woman consented to sex. The forensic expert for the defense used a linen handkerchief rubbed on the lawn where the rape was supposed to have taken place to show that a struggle would have produced grass stains on the woman's dress. The prosecutor challenged the use of linen because it was not the silky material of the dress. The forensic expert was reduced to defending his choice of linen based on his desire to preserve a costly dress. This defense technique

39

was not credible because trial expenses were known to be in the hundreds of thousands of dollars.

Site Orientation

Photographs, sketches, videotapes, and reports all help orient individuals to the accident scene. Such information allows experts to develop appropriate crisis explanations and to design related test and data taking procedures. It provides important clues to the state of the evidence and suggests what needs to be done to preserve and protect evidence. It helps with decisions concerning the reconstruction of damaged systems or the need to obtain exemplar systems. The inherent question is whether functional restoration of a damaged system or the comparability of form and function provided by a substitute will yield the most realistic test data.

A visit to a crisis site is often important because physical reality differs from visual, written, and spoken information. An expert needs to walk around to get a feel for the situation and to observe from different perspectives. Specialists need to focus on how the test data they will collect fits the analysis and crisis context. Site visits often affect the interpretations of accident facts and theories.

A nighttime accident involved a boat that rammed an anchored yacht. Witnesses stated the yacht had more than appropriate lighting for the circumstances. A site visit revealed that, from a boat perspective, the yacht was anchored in line with a bridge and a service road. At night, the yacht, although illuminated, disappeared into the background shore lighting. Photographs and videotapes of the scene did not show this situation.

Test Plans and Procedures

A test plan is useful because it establishes a common baseline for everyone involved. A test plan should describe the site and the situation; outline the purpose of the testing; assign individual responsibilities and interfaces; provide the test agenda;

indicate how the results of the test will be used; and help in controlling costs, schedules, and variations.

The test procedure provides the step-by-step implementation of the test plan. It should be prioritized and event driven to make sure the most important data related to the most probable explanation of an accident is collected first.

> *As part of reconstruction testing, an engine was operated at top speed to establish a performance maximum. The engine experienced a catastrophic mechanical failure which immediately negated the primary purpose of the test. Subsequent legal disagreements concerning discovery deadlines prevented retest and undermined plaintiff arguments.*

Under complicated circumstances involving numerous experts, test plans and procedures should be written and circulated to test participants to ensure they make sense and are complete. Testing should not proceed until understanding is achieved. Team members tend to defer to a team leader even though they don't understand or agree with the approach. It is particularly important to create an atmosphere of mutual respect allowing free and open interchange of ideas.

Test plans and procedures often result from the use of industry and government standards and practices. Tests based on a generally accepted and understood approach are preferable to specially designed tests more likely to be challenged as methodologically or scientifically unsound.

Checklists and Predefined Data Recording Forms

Checklists identify the instrumentation and equipment needed. Data recording forms simplify data taking under stress and environmental extremes. Forms for recording data should identify the types of tests to be done and should be organized and sequenced to reflect data-taking priorities. These forms should provide plenty of space for recording needed data and for writing comments so deviations or unusual circumstances can be noted. These forms should be easy to use and read.

Field testing of a boat had to be performed to beat a discovery deadline. Unfortunately, test conditions were terrible. The air and water temperatures were near freezing. The water was rough. A rain, snow, and sleet mixture fell intermittently throughout the day. Communication equipment did not work. The data was recorded using a waterproof pen on soggy paper.

Video and Still Cameras

Still and video cameras are now essential tools in testing. Photographs inexpensively record configuration and show the relationship between test instruments and the item to be tested. Video cameras record test dynamics and are particularly useful in operational timing, distance, and motion analyses.

The visual record of a test provides a sense of situation reality and exposes an audience to the context in which an incident occurred.

Field Instrumentation

Field instruments should be rugged and portable. They should be easily installed, used and read. Field instrument usage should meet, but not exceed, the needs of the situation. Technology considerations in the choice of such instruments are important because of cost and accuracy concerns. Care must be taken, however, to avoid substituting sophisticated instrumentation for test results.

Field test setup almost always takes longer than anticipated because of unexpected conditions. For example, damaged equipment and facilities functionally restored may have been physically altered. Field instruments, therefore, may not mount easily or may have to be placed in suboptimal locations.

Care should be exercised to eliminate bias in field testing. Instruments should be calibrated before testing and checked immediately after testing. Calibrated consumables should be appropriately used.

> *A yacht manufacturer was the defendant in a carbon monoxide death case. Testers working for the plaintiff attorney used a smoke bomb to show how the carbon monoxide could have flowed into the cabin of the boat. The smoke bomb, however, created pressures of far greater magnitude than any carbon monoxide leak. Subsequent testing provided a strong alternative theory of the accident: Atmospheric conditions accounted for the buildup of this toxic gas around the boat rather than in it. The $50 million lawsuit, which would have bankrupt the manufacturer, was subsequently settled for $500,000.*

Field testing is usually more representative of situation than laboratory testing, but requires greater flexibility and forgiveness to account for variations in field situations. Field testing, while less accurate than laboratory testing, is not less scientific. Good practice employs scientific method, and good scientific method involves recognition of the limits of testing and test equipment.

Laboratory Instrumentation

At times the condition or type of evidence, site limitations, or the need for precision precludes the use of field testing. The examination of microscopic quantities of evidence, the confirmation of special material properties, and the reconstruction of highly dangerous situations involving explosive, combustible, or toxic materials are examples of situations where laboratory testing under carefully controlled conditions is essential.

The expensive and sophisticated scientific instrumentation found in laboratories is operated and maintained by trained specialists working in controlled environments. The results of laboratory testing will almost certainly require interpretation by these individuals.

The positive side of laboratory testing is it provides exquisite control of precision and test environment. The negative side is that laboratory testing sometimes yields results that are or appear to be disconnected from reality.

> A technical specialist was hired to do a spectrometric analysis of particles found on a broken shaft. The laboratory test data indicated that the particles were not from the shaft and could not be correlated with material commonly used with the product. The resulting deposition testimony was ambiguous and confusing. The judge in the case excluded the deposition testimony and prevented the expert from appearing at trial.

Successful testing, whether field or laboratory, involves keeping activities simple and relevant to the situation.

Analysis

Analysis breaks down a problem into manageable parts. Analysis involves control of situation facts, definitions, boundaries, and concepts so that the realities and ambiguities of a crisis can be understood. For analysis to be effective, care must be taken to ensure that repeatable results are obtained.

Analysis normally involves trade-off studies that support risk assessment. Crisis analysis should be iterative in nature because information continuously flows into the analytical framework from tests, experts, and other sources. Iteration of the analysis clarifies and improves the quality of explanations. Analytical methods used must be verified and validated. Even generally accepted methodologies must be requalified for use in a specific situation. Importantly, a fact or finding that radically alters situation understanding may require changes to analytical methods and models.

Analysis is underpinned by science or practice, not fantasy or speculation.

Scientific Theory

The theories of science govern what is known about the universe. All practice evolves from the application of the hard sciences such as physics and chemistry, or from the soft sciences such as psychology and sociology. The real truth of a situation, whether discoverable or not, rests within the framework of science.

Analytical Processes Experts Use

Because it is generic and often abstract, science can be forgotten, twisted or ignored in the interrogation/testimony arena.

During a fatal boating accident, a steering arm mechanism was bent. At trial, the plaintiff attorney, contrary to the laws of motion and energy, argued this was the cause of the accident. The defense, however, was unable to convince the jury it was impossible for the mechanism to bend and initiate the accident. The defendant lost $700,000.

General Practice

Scientific theory has to be transformed into real-world use. Business or technical practices support this transformation by focusing science on problems and opportunities. Such practices ultimately become the basis for survival and success during a crisis and the turbulent period that follows.

Organizations that concentrate on continuous improvement and exceed industry or government standards are better able to defend themselves than organizations that merely meet the standard. Notably, a standard can have more than one interpretation. And what is perceived to be meeting an industry or government standard may not meet a jury standard.

Organizations should be customer conscious, pay attention to detail, and effectively integrate safety, performance, and quality to maximize the potential for success in the aftermath of a crisis.

The Disney enterprise has an unparalleled reputation for success in civil suits. The underlying defense involves Disney's famous attention to detail, concern for safety and security, and the squeaky clean image of Mickey Mouse.

Situation Reality

Situation reality is grounded in concrete evidence and organization information. Anomalies, however, are part of a crisis. Witnesses may differ over the facts. Evidence may be lost, misplaced or temporarily removed. Experts may make mistakes.

Instruments fail. It is these frailties, and probability rather than certainty, that lead to variations in conclusions and opinions.

By using theory, practice, evidence, and organization information, the expert hopes to discover the truth.

Analysis Methods and Results

Analysis attempts to understand but not duplicate the crisis situation. There is no way to perfectly recapture the past.

Analytical methods involve the development and use of a wide variety of frameworks, formulas, models, and simulations to achieve results.

Quantitative Analysis

Quantitative analysis is mathematics and data dependent. It addresses the right or wrong of crisis theories, practices, and situation understandings.

Quantitative analysis employs the universally accepted laws of the hard sciences. It is based on what is or was.

Quantitative analysis ensures that facts, not speculation, underpin interrogation/testimony arguments.

Qualitative Analysis

Qualitative analysis deals with contexts. It addresses better and worse explanations of a crisis rather than right or wrong. It uses tradeoffs to develop opinions based not only on facts but also on crisis ambiguity and complexity.

Qualitative analysis uses the theories of the soft sciences, such as psychology and sociology, to infer a logical finding. It is not restricted to what is or was, but can extend into what should be or should have been.

Qualitative analysis ensures that the normal context within which a crisis occurred is examined.

Analytical Results

The results of quantitative and qualitative analyses are used to understand and assess situation risks. Analysis results are key to organization and individual preparations for the interrogation/testimony dialogue. They provide feedback on the need for additional information gathering, testing, and resources. Improvements to product and process design and industrial competitiveness are often a beneficial spinoff from crisis analysis.

Challenges to Analysis

Analyses will be challenged in every imaginable way because discovered flaws can invalidate or weaken the usefulness of results. Assumptions and boundary conditions, definitions of terms, factual understandings, methodologies, relevance to situation, scientific and practical validity, and the impact of visual images must be defended.

Reviews

Reviews constitute good practice, and are appropriate for tracking and controlling the aftermath of a crisis. Reviews should be driven by key events rather than the calendar. An immediate post-crisis review, for example, should examine findings and lessons learned, address factual understandings and knowledge deficits, and begin the process of post-crisis planning. Reviews should also occur before and after major tests or demonstrations. Reviews should be tied to meeting externally imposed demands such as the filing of a civil suit or the taking of depositions.

Reviews provide excellent opportunities to address and readdress risks. An updated risk assessment should be part of the review agenda.

Risk Assessment

In the interrogation/testimony environment, the negative aspects of prior decisions and actions are substantially magnified. General benefits, even if overwhelmingly positive, can be lost in the spotlight of intense criticism.

Risk assessments are done as part of the development of products or services. All too often, however, the thorough assessment used to identify normal-use risks discount misuse and abuse.[8] The presumption is consumers will use a product for the purpose intended and are responsible for risks beyond those *normally* foreseeable. Unfortunately, this thinking does not suffice in an adversarial situation because known or easily anticipated misuses and abuses are often *reasonably* foreseeable.

If the risk of use, abuse or misuse can be eliminated through design and manufacturing activity, action should be taken to change existing designs and possibly to recall products that have been placed in the stream of commerce. If redesign or remanufacture to eliminate a potentially hazardous condition is not possible, then guarding devices or monitoring systems should be employed. Customer training, in combination with guarding devices and monitoring systems, may be effective in reducing the number, type, or severity of accidents. As a final reminder, written or visual warnings should be used.

Post-crisis risk assessments deal with mitigation of the impact of the crisis and point toward regaining organization and individual stability. Such assessments should define and evaluate a number of best, most probable, and worst-case results, and should suggest modification of crisis management activities to reduce liabilities.

Fundamentally, risk is defined by probability of occurrence and severity of consequence. Low risks do not deserve special attention as they are part of normal day-to-day business activity. Moderate risks deserve investment based on priorities and the availability of resources. High risks demand investment. Risk handling involves avoidance, control, assumption, and transference of risk. An effective risk assessment links crisis objectives to decision making.

One final note on risk assessment: Organizations tend to think in terms of internal risks which they can control. Crises are inherently external events and can be only partially mitigated by

---

[8] All too often, a manufacturer claims ignorance of product or process misuse even though corporate articles and pictures clearly show the misuse. Furthermore, the primary problem that causes misuse or abuse is almost certain to have industry-wide recognition.

organization or individual activity. Risk assessments should be consumer oriented.

Decision Making

Decision making must relate to organization and crisis objectives. It must consider crisis demands and costs within the framework of normal organization operations. It must be influenced by preservation of reputation, stability of organization, and survival. Any decision should complement individual preparations.

Good decision making in a crisis requires commitment to action. It must be oriented toward relieving the physical, mental, and emotional problems of people affected by the crisis.

Summary

Within this chapter a logical analytical process that supports crisis decision making was outlined. Analysis provides the factual and logical basis for answers. Analysis quality, therefore, is based on care in the use of information, evidence, and test results.

Analysis requires that theory and appropriate practice be comprehensively applied to the realities of a situation. All aspects of analysis must be thoroughly dissected during reviews because rigorous challenges to validity will be encountered. All of this expensive, time-consuming activity leads to a risk assessment which ties decision making to crisis objectives.

In the next chapter, discussion will focus on individual preparations.

Pre-Interrogation Expert Preparations

Overview

Thorough preparation makes the expert a mentally tough yet reasonable human being who can make optimal use of knowledge, experience, and communication skills. Success or failure in the interrogation/testimony environment is related to the quality of preparation activity.

Discussion in this chapter will focus on preparations for testifying. Of specific interest is knowing objectives, positions and roles; gaining command of information; using pre-briefs to prepare; and stage setting.

Know Objectives, Positions, and Roles

In the interrogation/testimony environment, it is important to understand organization and professional objectives, to know individual roles, and to appreciate the reasons behind an appearance.

Have or Know the Objective

An individual, acting on behalf of himself or herself, a position, or an organization, should be focused on objectives that complement short- and long-term crisis management.

In a damage control situation, for example, an organization's *short-term* objectives would involve limiting the extent of the crisis and convincing adversely affected people the organization is responding rapidly and effectively. The spokesperson for the organization would outline how the organization was bringing all available resources to bear, and would act as the central source for information disclosure. Other knowledgeable corporate personnel would indicate a personal and professional commitment to act responsibly. Speculation, however, about what happened and what long-term actions would be taken should be avoided.

Long-term damage control objectives would involve assessing the risks of litigation, legislation, criminal prosecution, and unfavorable media exposure, as well as cleanup, restoration, and future use. Individuals involved in meeting such long-term objectives must weigh organizational, professional, and personal objectives. Long-term organizational objectives should normally be fully supported as long as they are within legal limits. Unfortunately, such support is not always possible because corporate activities can be within the law but still unethical. An individual whose design is blamed for an incident can be personally as well as corporately liable. And professional credentials essential to future employment can be threatened. Conflicts occur when information is withheld under legal privilege or for proprietary reasons.

As noted previously, organization objectives are not limited to damage control only. Through individual representatives, organizations often go public to promote or affirm a particular position even if the position is clearly disliked by a substantial number of people. Positive arguments should dominate, although not to the extent of dishonest, unreasonable, or ridiculous advocacy.

> *President Clinton's 1993 tax increase was unpopular with the American electorate. Nevertheless, he was able to squeak it through Congress by being a positive, energetic spokesman for increased taxation as part of an overall deficit-reduction strategy. A positive image, persistence, and a*

strong dose of compromise were the basis for winning a contentious legislative battle.

Objectives can also involve combating unfair media exposés, unsubstantiated litigation, and biased analyses damaging to a reputation. Individuals supporting fairness objectives should appeal to an audience's sense of justice by providing an overwhelming set of facts and analyses to discredit opposing positions. Truth and fairness campaigns should deal in reality and strongly and aggressively criticize fantasy, speculation, and outright fraud.

General Motors lost over $100 million as a result of a jury verdict in a wrongful death case. A media exposé, showing the explosive reality of a side-impact crash into a GM truck, further damaged the organization's reputation. General Motors, however, discovered the tests from the exposé had been unfairly rigged to sensationalize the story. GM protested the network's use of unfair and unethical tactics and threatened to remove all advertising. The network apologized and disciplined the investigative reporters and executives involved.

Inherent in any crisis is both a problem and an opportunity. Crisis-related objectives should reflect both, and individuals involved in crisis management should be prepared to reduce losses and exploit gains. For example, a chemical spill may be immediately disastrous; however, collaboration between hazardous-materials cleanup crews, and the organization's initial investigation team could demonstrate good emergency preparedness.

One additional note: Individuals must be free to ask about and challenge objectives. Ambiguous, confusing, or hard-to-believe objectives often cause individuals to make inadvertent statements that create additional conflicts and problems and misrepresent important issues and positions. Individual preparations require clear communication.

Don't Assume Knowledge

Even the most knowledgeable individuals often have time-sensitive information and positions allied to but not necessarily consistent with current crisis management thinking. Positions are often time dependent, and differences among past reports, current status, and future plans are likely. Technical information comparisons will often expose design and manufacturing compromises, test inadequacies, lack of knowledge and experience, and outright mistakes. Business information comparisons may reveal lack of progress, a cost increase for less work, and contract execution problems.

When time permits, defined positions should be the basis for interrogation/testimony discussion. This ensures answers will support organization objectives and, therefore, receive organization support. If current positions are not available or are still in formulation, the reasons for delay should be stated. It is acceptable and probably prudent to say, "I don't know" when the situation is in doubt.

Knowledge should not be used inflexibly. Individuals should be aware of major alternatives affecting the position they will represent. Part of the use of knowledge is to know how changes affect it. When the question "What if . . ." is posed by an interrogator, analytical positions should shift to what is reasonable under the new, speculative conditions.

Know the Role

In adversarial situations, roles vary from expert to fact witness to decision maker. Fact witnesses are not expected to speculate but to state what they know. Experts are expected to venture opinions based on education, experience, credentials, and appropriate analysis. Decision makers are expected to make commitments to a course of action.

In organizations, know the role involves coordination with the crisis management focal point to ensure the role makes sense and is compatible with short- and long-term organization concerns. During crises, however, individuals often assume expanded roles which extend their authority or expertise beyond reasonable limits.

> In 1981, immediately after an assassination attempt against President Ronald Reagan, Secretary of State Alexander Haig indicated he was in command at the White House. He was probably correct at the time, but by appearing to assume the constitutional powers of the President, he exceeded his legal authority.

Individuals preparing to testify should recognize their roles differ from the one associated with normal business activity. An individual's position in the organization may be of little significance in a situation driven by knowledge and image.

Know the Reason for Appearing

Individuals are used in interrogation/testimony situations for a variety of reasons. Individuals having little knowledge are used to minimize exposure to questions or to get a sense of adversarial positions and approaches before the real experts appear. Conversely, individuals with substantial expertise are used to support and articulate overwhelmingly logical and favorable positions or to undercut the reasonableness of opposing arguments.

Individuals are sometimes used as sacrificial lambs. Individuals who do not know why they are there, what their roles are, or what expectations the organization has for their performance, are in trouble.

Regardless of the reason for appearing, it is important to tell the truth and to put the best face forward. This involves advocating analytically powerful positions, operating cautiously when the pros and cons of the situation are not clear, and maintaining a defensive but not evasive stance when unfavorable issues are discussed.

Figure 3 depicts the relationship between objectives, knowledge, roles, and reasons for appearing. Notably, objectives provide the platform for success while knowledge, roles, and reasons for appearing are the pillars.

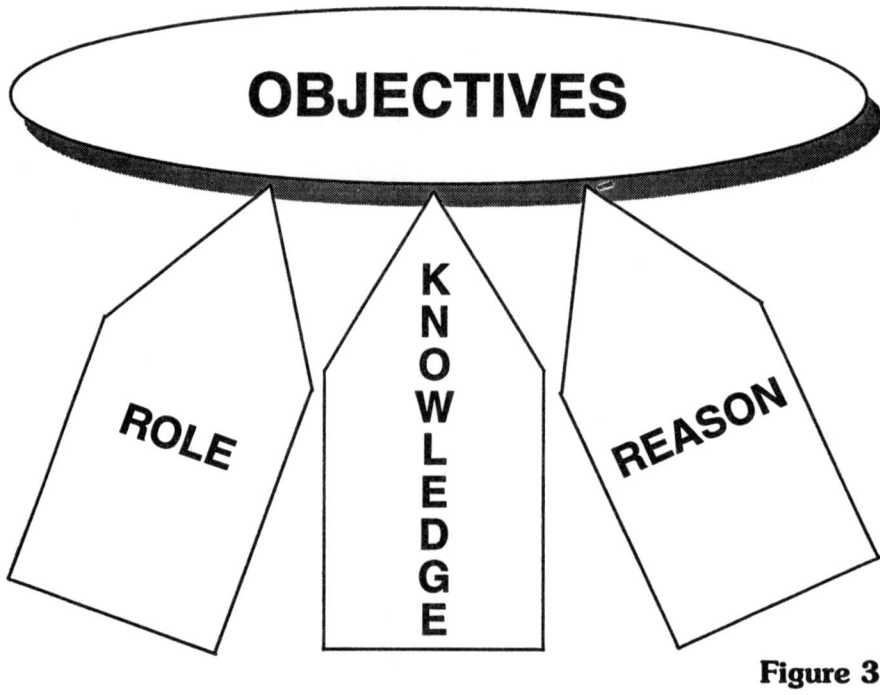

Figure 3

Gain Command of the Information

All too often the deposition transcripts or videotapes of executives, managers, and technical specialists reflect minimal preparation. Lack of preparation is sometimes based on the inherent nature of a crisis. Far too often, however, it is a display of arrogance or anger that gets translated during the interrogation/testimony dialogue into lack of caring, ignorance of corporate products or services, stupidity, or worse. In an adversarial situation, lack of preparation can be devastating as organization weaknesses are exposed and amplified and strengths are buried in incoherent and poorly constructed answers. Risks increase substantially as opportunities to resolve issues favorably, preserve financial stability, and maintain individual and corporate credibility and reputation are damaged or lost.

The expert should obtain the most current information and relate it to crisis objectives, strategies, and plans.

Situation Orientation

An emergency or crisis demands immediate attention and people need basic answers to orient themselves. Simple questions like "What is going on?" "What do we know?" "What do we say?" "Who is running the show and will make decisions?" and "How are we responding?" must be answered, or knowledge voids will be filled by speculation. Unfortunately, early speculation often becomes the organization's position even though subsequent information and evidence do not support it. Speculation should be avoided to reduce conflict and embarrassment.

It is important to recognize that the initial crisis orientation depends on readily available expertise and information. There simply is no time for thorough file searches and detailed studies. Evidence is unavailable because a systematic investigation of the crisis scene has not been possible. This limited information baseline plus incoming reports must be controlled so situation changes are communicated appropriately to crisis participants.

An effective orientation ensures short-term problems are expeditiously handled and long-term consequences are manageable with a minimum of confusion and contradiction.

Prepared Positions

Preparation for a media interview, deposition, or hearing usually rests on a set of specific positions that constitute the basis for most answers. In some instances, position papers will be developed and given directly to the media and other interested parties. Individuals to be interviewed should read the position papers thoroughly, not only because they constitute the basis for answers, but also because they may be confusing, contradictory, or inadequate.

Facts and Analyses

The expert should make sure the facts and analysis are comprehensible. Complex situations are not only difficult to explain but they may also be difficult to understand even for an expert. Effective communication requires that an expert clarify, not complicate, the situation for a jury or audience. A number of problems impact the effective use of information. Large amounts of information can obscure the essence of an argument or position. What was clearly understood a month or a year ago may now be a muddled maze. A written version of testimony will not account for nonverbal give and take. Simple, straightforward communications during depositions or interviews help to overcome these problems.

If understanding facts and analyses is important, understanding how the facts were collected and analyses done is also important. It is likely that data collection and analytical methodologies will be challenged to determine if basic or interpretive flaws exist. If an expert extrapolates, such extrapolation must be firmly grounded in technique, practice, and logic. If the extrapolation is unsupported or of obviously limited situation value, related testimony is undermined.

> *The O.J. Simpson criminal case was an example of the "leave no stone unturned" philosophy of top-line professional interrogators. Each piece of evidence, evidence collection and processing procedures, and even the evidence collectors themselves were challenged.*

Visual Aids

The use of visual aids requires mechanical and electrical know-how and an understanding of how such aids support the presentation of arguments. An air of confidence is created when the video is started and stopped appropriately, when drawing overlays show a logical step-by-step explanation of events, and when a simulation enlivens and clarifies the situation. Visual aids, however, should not become a crutch.

> *In a rush to complete discovery, an attorney accepted the scheduling of depositions before all pertinent information was available. At an expert's deposition, a videotape*

that had not been previewed was used. The expert had no idea what he was looking at or how it fit into his prior fact-finding testing activity. The result was an embarrassed expert and defensive testimony.

Know the Interrogator

Professional interrogators have styles and represent, knowingly or unknowingly, personal as well as professional interests. It is appropriate for an expert to garner information, preferably a biography and a sense of questioning tendencies, on the individual who will be a professional opponent during the interrogation/testimony dialogue. Personal knowledge enhances the expert's response because it suggests familiar examples and analogies that will ease and clarify communications. Fumbling questions and the confused answers that often result may then be avoided.

Prebriefs

A number of powerful communication enhancement mechanisms help individuals prepare to testify. The mock interview and murder board are common business practice. The preinterrogation chit chat is the informal start to the interrogation/testimony dialogue.

Mock Interviews

It is typical for attorneys to prepare their witnesses by subjecting them to the interrogation and inquiry tactics common to the legal profession. This gives the attorney a sense of how well an individual thinks and reacts to pressure and also what a particular response to a question will be.

The mock interview reveals the flow of questions and ideas; and in the case of the direct examination at trial, represents an understanding between the attorney and the expert on presentation dynamics and sequences. A mock interview also helps with the anticipation of opposing questions, although the sequence of such questions will not be known in advance.

An effective mock interview process carried through into a trial enhances situation control and creates the impression of a hard-working, dedicated team approach to testimony preparation. An ineffective mock interview can lead to a disjointed presentation of arguments and unpleasant surprises.

> *The night before trial an expert underwent a thorough mock interrogation. The attorney and the expert had resolved all issues of concern and were comfortable with the approaching trial presentation. Sometime after the mock interrogation, the attorney came up with a brainstorm and did not tell the expert about it. During the trial, this brainstorm appeared as one of the first questions of the direct examination. The question "How big is a boat?" startled everyone in the courtroom. The judge's reaction was something like "That is the dumbest question I have ever heard." Fortunately, the expert, although obviously disconcerted, had a good answer. The judge then said, "That was an excellent answer to a stupid question." The attorney did his client no good; he embarrassed himself and left his expert wondering what surprise would be next.*

It is not unusual during the mock interview for an attorney to suggest an answer favoring an advocated position. An expert will have to negotiate a response which is reasonable and defensible rather than accept an unsupportable answer. Unreasoned or excessive advocacy during the real interrogation/testimony dialogue causes loss of credibility and may constitute an untruth.

Murder Boards

It is common practice in the business community for managers to brief higher-level authorities. These managers often use teams of experts to help develop briefings and to test the effectiveness of a briefing before it is given. The murder board is often brutal as positions are vigorously debated, presentation flaws are exposed, and questions are asked that expose incomplete thinking and inadequate answers.

The individual undergoing a murder board must be able to accept blunt constructive criticism without getting embarrassed or hostile. If this individual is being prepared by lower-level specialists, rank and privilege should be left outside the door and a free-for-all dialogue encouraged. It is very important that all murder board comments be respected and appreciated because an ineffective murder board leads to unanticipated presentation problems.

Chit Chat

On some rare occasions, the interrogator and the expert get an opportunity to meet prior to the actual interview itself. The expert should use this opportunity to test the experience, intellect, and skills of the interrogator. It should not be used to talk about the subject matter because that may suggest additional damaging questions. It is important to realize that the friendly, even likable person involved in polite conservation may very soon become the aggressive, nasty antagonist when the real dialogue starts.

Stage Setting

An individual who undergoes interrogation is exposed to considerable stress. There is a powerful and continuous demand to think quickly and communicate effectively while under pressure. Under these conditions, it is important to minimize physical stress. If at all possible, the expert should select the place where the interrogation will occur. It should be made as physically comfortable as possible by adjusting lighting, window shades, temperature, cameras, microphones, and seating. Water and other supplies, such as paper and pencils, tissues, and snacks should be readily available, even within arm's reach. Administrative support personnel should be on call.

If the interrogation takes place in a neutral, unknown site, it is important for the expert to arrive early to get good parking (or take a taxi) and to become familiar with the facility layout. Restrooms, telephones, eating facilities, and water fountains should be located. Secretaries, security personnel, and others who have an official capacity at the site should be asked about facility do's and don'ts and process etiquette. If possible, the expert should select the most comfortable, conducive spot for the interrogation. Just prior to the start of the formal interrogation, the expert should adjust microphones to allow eye contact with the audience, look for friendly faces to talk to, get water in order to drink and think, and adjust chairs, podiums, and equipment.

> *In one memorably funny situation, experts who were lecturing an interest group audience ranged widely in height. Even though the podium was adjustable and the microphone removable, nobody touched the equipment, preferring instead to perform physical contortions for 30 to 45 minutes at a time.*

An interrogation taking place at the opposition's site must be presumed to be staged to create as much physical pressure as possible. It is not unusual for a witness to be interrogated in a warm (or cold) room with poor lighting and uncomfortable chairs. Notably, an expert undergoing interrogation is entitled to professional courtesy. The proceedings should not begin until reasonable conditions are provided.

Interrogations often take place at times that disrupt normal habits. Trials may begin as late as 10:00 A.M. and the judge may not recess for lunch until 12:30 or 1:00 P.M. A 6:00 A.M. breakfast does not last until 12:30 P.M. and the resulting hunger pangs and associated noises disrupt thought processes. To compensate for these time shifts, some crackers and a stimulating beverage should be consumed during recesses.

Media interrogations often occur at the site of a crisis where it is difficult to find a quiet place to reflect upon and analyze the situation. A familiarization tour, restroom and energy replenishment breaks, or some diversion will probably be needed to buy time before an interrogation begins.

Summary

This chapter addressed the steps an expert should take to prepare for the interrogation/testimony dialogue. At this juncture, individual roles should be defined; the factual and analytical basis for testifying should be understood; the objectives should be known; the positions to be discussed and their alternatives should be clear; and the site for the interrogation should be determined and explored. The expert is now fair game.

In the next few chapters, discussion will focus on the pressures of testifying. First and foremost, the audience is viewed as a collection of decision makers. Next comes the interrogator who is in charge of the questions. Finally, the expert witness enters the stage as the individual with the answers.

The Audience, The Interrogator, and The Expert Witness

Overview

The first steps into the limelight of the interrogation/testimony arena are often nervous and fearful ones. Individuals stumble over their names and addresses, become confused and disoriented by the magnitude of the situation, and experience the symptoms of physical stress. Stage fright is normal and expected. After all, the expert witness is very much like an actor in an improvisation theater.

The interrogation/testimony stage is not just the facility in which adversarial dialogue takes place. It also contains script materials made from information, evidence, testing, and analysis; and scenery composed of crisis images. The primary actors in the play are the interrogators and expert witnesses. The cast includes among others, judges, support personnel, and clients. The most important part of the play, however, is the audience, jury, interest group, or decision maker. The "battle on the stage of life" is for the hearts and minds of these less-than-perfect human beings.

Discussion in this chapter will focus on an interrogator skilled in inquiry, an expert witness with the facts and analyses, and an audience of concerned human beings.

Under Pressure

Pressure can be controlled but not avoided. It is an inherent and, at times, oppressive part of the adversarial environment. Individuals who have experienced depositions, the glaring lights of the media, the government hearing, the audit, or the "in-your-face" screams of interest groups know that reasonableness is difficult to maintain; and that truth is, at times, nearly impossible to communicate.

The expert witness must function effectively regardless of the type and intensity of pressure. Considerable self discipline is needed to absorb assaults on ego and remain committed and motivated to articulating arguments. Unfortunately, self protection is one of the most substantive reasons for loss of control in the interrogation/testimony dialogue.

During a deposition, a military officer was asked when he had his last psychiatric exam. This question caused him to respond emotionally because it attacked his sense of self worth, professionalism, and competence. More importantly, it undermined his ability to respond effectively to subsequent questions. He confused legitimate adversarial pressure with a personal attack.

Professionally designed adversarial criticism intended to damage and destroy is unique and unusual. To respond effectively to such criticism, the expert witness must be deliberate, objective, and dispassionate. However, interrogator diatribes or obvious and deliberate abuse should not go unchallenged.

The Audience

The audience is the most important element in the interrogation/testimony arena. It is the audience that decides right or wrong, good or bad, and ultimately, who wins and loses. To function effectively, an audience must develop a sense of fairness, justice, and comfort with the ultimate decision.

Audiences may be neutral, friend, or foe. Regardless of initial orientation, however, an audience can be persuaded through honest, professional communications that show why the positions represented are reasonable and logical.

The Neutral Audience

If the orientation of the audience is not known, it is presumed to be neutral—neither particularly interested or disinterested in the result. Most juries, for example, are not personally or economically affected by who wins or loses a civil suit or criminal proceeding. The interrogation/testimony dialogue, therefore, centers on converting this audience to favor one side or the other.

It is important to note that a neutral audience is treating arguments equally and doing an objective analysis to support its decision making. The expert witness who best supports this effort through a simple, straightforward presentation will be viewed favorably. Conversely, the expert witness who delves into minutia or goes off on exquisite tangents will probably lose such an audience, even though the position supported is logically and analytically stronger.

Neutral audiences are open to reasonable appeals and are not to be blamed for inadequate understanding. Many audiences, even though technologically unsophisticated, can reason quite well if led step by step through a complicated process. The expert who says, "Those dumb people did not understand" is to be blamed for ineffective communications and improper audience education. No audience can be expected to know as much as the expert witness.

> *Ross Perot used flip charts in his infomercials to clearly and understandably articulate problems with the federal deficit and debt. Each chart made a simple point that could be easily grasped. The charts were logically sequenced so cause and effect could be understood. Perot encouraged the audience to see positive and negative trends and assess the bottom-line impact of the overall presentation.*

Neutral audiences are swayed point by point, but won by the total weight of a reasoned argument. To affect decision making, key points must be continuously emphasized within the context of the argument. A single point may win an exchange, but its importance will be dissipated by time or lack of context. Friendly or unfriendly audiences often dwell exclusively on points supporting their version of the argument, but neutral audiences have no preconceived notions.

Friendly Audiences

To look and feel good, politicians pick friendly audiences. A large group of smiling faces reduces pressure because basic agreement can be assumed and confrontation is unlikely. The friendly audience is a source of positive power that invigorates and energizes. It provides an appreciation of past actions and an affirmation for likely future decisions.

> *Going into the 1992 Republican national convention, President George Bush looked like a tired man. The obvious affection of most Republicans for the successes of the Bush presidency, in particular the war against Iraq, clearly enlivened him in his attempt to be a second-term President.*

With friendly audiences, expert witnesses can say and do almost anything. Statements and gestures that might be silly or offensive in other forums support a relaxed comfortable atmosphere. In dealing with friendly audiences, however, it is important to maintain control, stay within expected limits, and avoid surprises. Friendly audiences can be rapidly turned off by stupidity or obvious ignorance.

Unfriendly Audiences

It is not unusual for the expert witness to be confronted simultaneously by both interrogators and unfriendly audiences. Interrogators will exaggerate the negatives to stimulate such an audience. An unfriendly audience will seldom become friendly, preferring instead to blame argument failure on the messenger, system, or situation rather than their core beliefs.

> In Inherit the Wind, a play about the criminal prosecution of a teacher who introduced the theory of evolution into the Southern Bible Belt, attorney Clarence Darrow represented evolution. During the play (and the actual prosecution), Darrow was able to get his attorney opponent, William Jennings Bryan, to take the witness stand as an expert on the biblical version of creation. During direct examination, Darrow undermined Bryan on fundamental issues of Biblical interpretation. The impact on the unfriendly jury and courtroom audience was stunning. People who had been cheering Bryan and hooting at Darrow retreated into silence and sullen acceptance of loss. In fact and fiction, Bryan never recovered his equanimity or credibility.

Feedback from an unfriendly audience is often immediate, insulting, and bullying. Unfriendly audiences may not be there to hear the truth but simply to vent emotions. In such situations, an expert witness should try to remain dignified and reasonable. If this is not possible and the situation appears threatening or impossibly unproductive, a graceful exit is appropriate.

In dealing with unfriendly audiences, it may be best to acknowledge difficulties and adversity. This approach is essentially an appeal to reason and humanity—individual to individual rather than individual to group. If rapport can be established with even a few individuals, a reasonable discourse might eventually take place.

Audience Tendencies and Limits

Another dimension to audience persuasion should be noted here. Audiences are made up of different races, sexes, ages, religions, and ethnicity. These differences affect listening and individual learning styles. For example, American women are probably listening when they nod their heads and maintain eye contact, while American men do the opposite and may even appear to be

69

distracted. Also, women's questions are most often designed to elicit more information, while men's questions are designed to analyze.[9]

Attorneys take group sociological tendencies to the personal level by hiring psychologists to help pick juries. The presumption is that individuals, consciously or subconsciously, provide written, verbal, and nonverbal clues to their objectivity and their openness to persuasion and reason.

Some audiences, specifically juries, are given formal limits. A judge, for example, will charge a jury to consider certain types of information in specific ways or, conversely, to ignore improperly presented information. An expert witness must be careful to stay within these limits or face disrupted and potentially excluded testimony.

The Interrogator

The interrogator is the initiator of the action and most are well prepared to articulate pertinent, probing questions. The expert witness should assume that any interrogator operating in the interrogation/testimony arena is a competent professional.

The Interrogator Controls the Questions

First and foremost, the interrogator controls the questions. The expert witness should not challenge a question other than to indicate that it is unclear or does not make sense. The expert witness who interprets the question is merely giving the interrogator another question to ask and is increasing overall testimonial risk.

Interrogators are experts in the interrogation process. A good interrogator prepares thoroughly and knows the facts, analyses, alternatives, and risks. An expert witness, however, should not mistake logical sentences, good interrogation skills, and a sense of understanding for technical expertise and knowledge.

---

[9] Information on male/female dynamics is available from the Jayne Tear Group in New York, NY

Thorough interrogator preparation improves the quality of the interview or dialogue. It provides a good intellectual test and clarifies many aspects of opposing positions. A well-thought-out, focused question solicits the best from an expert witness because it concentrates on specifics and demands a response equal in clarity to the question. Conversely, poorly prepared questions are often ambiguous and confusing to everyone.

> During cross examination, a young attorney asked a hypothetical question containing many clauses and taking nearly three minutes to read. The expert witness was confused in trying to sort out clause relationships and grammatical conflicts. He turned to the trial judge and indicated the question was incomprehensible. The judge ordered the question reread. The expert answered, "No!" The attorney showed surprise and consternation, and the silence that followed indicated to everybody in the courtroom that the attorney did not understand the question and had no follow up.

Interrogators usually organize questions to reflect priorities and important themes. Good interrogators, however, are flexible and adapt to changes so they can amplify argument strengths and minimize weaknesses. Poor interrogators tend to jump around in a disorganized fashion. Such behavior often reflects lack of knowledge, inadequate preparation, and uncertainty.

The Interrogator Does Not Control the Answers

The interrogator has the right to establish the scope of the inquiry and to use interrogation tactics in the pursuit of understanding and advantage. The interrogator does not, however, have the right to provide the answers.

The expert witness should be wary of questions that seek only agreement or disagreement. In such questions, language usage is defined by the interrogator and may, therefore, ultimately lead to contradiction or even perverse agreement with an opposed argument.

Is Not the Audience

The interrogator is not the audience! The interrogator is not the audience! The interrogator is not the audience! This should be drummed into the psyche of every expert witness because assuming the opposite is the most common and potentially the most damaging mistake that can be made.

An expert witness competes with the interrogator for audience attention, interest, and sympathy. Figure 4 depicts the interaction between the interrogator and expert witness to influence audience decision making.

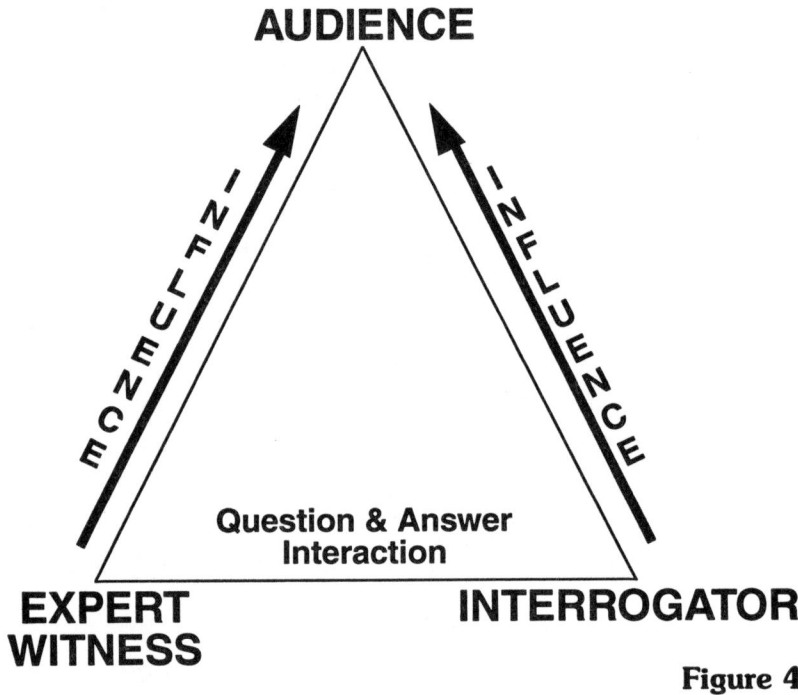

Figure 4

The Expert Witness

Expert witnesses react to the questions asked by interrogators. They do not compete with the interrogator except to support audience understanding and decision making.

The Expert Witness Controls the Answers

First and foremost, answers are supported by facts and analyses. Expert witnesses, therefore, must provide a rationale for conclusions and opinions. They should not give in to intimidation that undermines the truth.

In the interrogation/testimony dialogue, individuals tend to ramble on. The expert witness, however, should control the answer and stop when finished. Excessively wordy answers confuse an audience. Such answers also undermine credibility, introduce unintended contradictions, and lead to speculation. It is important to note that if the answer is insufficient, another question will be asked to ensure understanding, or some future question can be used to fill in recognized gaps.

Many people do not like silence or long pauses, and interrogators may pause to see if silence will solicit more information. Sometimes the pause reflects indecision or confusion.

During a deposition, an attorney asked a garbled question. In the silence that followed, the expert witness became uncomfortable and decided to respond anyway. The subsequent set of questions and answers became so confused the expert finally had to admit he had not made sense to the attorney or to himself. This was embarrassing at the time, and a year later had to be explained during trial because the answers appeared to contradict previous testimony. Silence should be treated as an opportunity to think.

Finally, if examples and analogies are used as part of an answer, keep them simple and tailor them to the audience.

The Expert Witness Does Not Control the Questions

The interrogator does not control the answer and should not be allowed to control it. Conversely, the expert witness does not, and therefore should not, attempt to control the question. Acts by expert witnesses to control questions seldom succeed because they open up unexpected and, therefore, uncontrollable lines of inquiry. Clever interrogators will often provide incomplete or partial questions and wait for the respondent to read into the question.

Questions do tend to follow certain tracks and themes. The expert witness, therefore, can often anticipate where a sequence of questions is leading. Anticipation must be controlled, however, because an interrogator may deliberately and suddenly shift the topics to catch the unwary.

Boredom and distraction reduce the expert witness' ability to concentrate. It is especially easy to lose track of questions at the end of a long and tiring day. If distraction has occurred, ask for the question to be repeated. Do not assume understanding or wing it based on what may have been heard.

It is critically important to concentrate on and answer the question at hand. It is responsive, reasonable, and prudent.

Influence of the Expert Witness

The expert witness is a communicator, educator, and image maker. Unfortunately, to be professional and demonstrate competence, expert witnesses have a tendency to answer questions inflexibly and use overly complicated words, phrases, and examples. In attempts to be objective, they may appear arrogant and disinterested or become detached from the issues.

> *A number of years ago, one of the major television news shows interviewed a State Department counter-terrorism expert. As the interview unfolded it became obvious that this individual never blinked or smiled. By the end of the interview, one was left with the impression that the man was remorseless and inhuman. The audience lost track of the argument as a result.*

The expert witness must remember there is a human message to be conveyed to a human audience.

Summary

In this chapter, the three key elements of the interrogation/testimony arena: the audience, the interrogator, and the expert witness were addressed.

The audience is the most important element in this arena because they make decisions and form lasting opinions that translate into individual and organization wins and losses. The interrogator is responsible for the quality and clarity of questions. The expert witness is responsible for truthful answers. Each of these role distinctions must be scrupulously observed.

In the next chapter, discussion will focus on expert witness responsibilities and expectations. Issues affecting truth, credibility, and results will be explored. The impact of mistakes and emotions will also be addressed.

Expert Witness Responsibilities  VII

Overview

The interrogation/testimony dialogue is obviously unique. The expert witness, therefore, has a distinct set of responsibilities and expectations to fulfill when answering questions. The truth must not be abused. Attention to detail in the development and presentation of evidence, information, and images is required. Credibility, which evolves from professional competence and integrity, contributes to success but does not guarantee a winning result.

Mistakes and emotions are part of the adversarial process. The expert witness must be a reasonable, not perfect human being.

Discussion in this chapter will focus on the core responsibilities of the expert witness.

Presentation: Answering Questions is Not Enough

The expert witness reacts to questions and tries to answer them in a truthful manner. Obsessive adherence to an interrogator's preferences or preimposed constraints, however, is not appropriate because it does not account for the adversarial context and may not meet the needs of an audience. Answering questions requires that an expert witness understand the impact of time and sequence in the presentation of facts and ideas, and the appropriate use of language and visual information. Fundamentally, an expert witness answering questions must be a communicator, educator, and image maker.

Communicator

The good communicator tries to provide an easy-to-understand message. The expert witness must effectively communicate while being subject to conflicting and harassing questions.

> *During the gulf war, General Colin Powell, Chairman of the Joint Chiefs of Staff, used clear and concise sentences, good diction, and command bearing to communicate with the American people about Iraqi war efforts. His presentation style conveyed a sense of military professionalism and power. General Powell also teamed very effectively with Secretary of Defense Richard Cheney to answer questions on military progress and defense policy. Each man clearly represented a different role, yet both provided the expertise to answer a broad range of military and political questions. By observing role distinctions, Cheney and Powell had numerous opportunities to "get off stage" and think through key themes and positions to be communicated.*

The expert witness can have a strong and compelling set of factual and analytical arguments and not communicate effectively. Emotional outbursts, speculative gibberish, overly complex and detailed responses, or poor grammar or language skills can cause confusion and loss of credibility.

In the legal environment, the expert witness should adapt to meet the needs of the jury. An attentive jury normally indicates the expert witness is communicating effectively. It does not, however, reflect agreement with the message. A distracted restless jury often signals trouble with communication. It is not unusual for an expert witness to find both attentive and inattentive individuals in a jury box. An attentive individual may be signaling physical attraction, appreciation for the effort, or agreement. An inattentive individual may be bored, disinterested, or already convinced. If given a choice, the expert witness should target communication to people who are paying attention because they have the best chance of understanding the message and using it during decision-making deliberations.

Educator

The good educator starts with, talks to, and ends on what is important. The expert witness should repeat key points and positions for an audience because they are much like students in a classroom being exposed to new information and ideas. (Memory is selective and retention is based on what is emphasized.)

The expert witness should simplify complex situations by laying out an easily understood analytical framework and fitting evidence and information into that framework in brief and precise segments. This is particularly important when dealing with a jury whose decisions are binding on plaintiffs and defendants. Disconnected points, even though individually compelling, are less than the sum of the whole. A well-organized but weaker argument can therefore carry the day.

> *An attorney and expert witness can form a very effective educational team. One case involved a boating accident that cost the plaintiff both legs and the loss of sexual function. Prior to trial the attorney closely coordinated the photographic information with the expert. The subsequent staged courtroom presentation was a highly professional, step-by-step education about how the design flaws of the boat contributed to the accident. The jury delivered a multimillion dollar verdict for the severely injured plaintiff.*

Ultimately, an expert witness brings an audience to a level of understanding that allows them to be comfortable with and confident in their decision.

Image Maker

Images are an important part of an expert witness' presentation. Images can dominate facts and change decisions.

> *In the criminal case against Mayor Marion Barry of Washington, DC, the facts were not in dispute. A hidden video camera had recorded his usage of cocaine. His attorney effectively attacked the criminal prosecution by creating an image of a ruthless federal government deliberately targeting and abusing an African-American leader. The mayor was subsequently acquitted of all felony charges and only served time for a misdemeanor.*

The expert witness should strongly consider using multimedia presentation capabilities to organize and depict complex issues. A dynamic multimedia presentation allows the expert witness to break crisis sequences into understandable parts and to focus on and repeat those parts that are most relevant to a specific argument. It can also minimize problems that arise from cultural and linguistic diversity. Photographs, videotapes, and simulations, however, should accurately reflect reality, contribute to understanding the truth of the situation, and not be prejudicial.

Fundamentally, many choices and methods are available to convey a message, and to ensure questions are answered effectively.

The Truth

The expert witness must tell the truth, but be reasonable about it. In most crisis situations, the truth is only partially known and depends on interpretation. Plaintiff arguments in lawsuits often stress "what should have been," while defense arguments emphasize "what was reasonable" at a point in time. Absolute statements that reflect certainty under such murky circumstances will be quickly challenged. Furthermore, absolute statements with a limited factual basis may prove to be mistaken.

Several friends were hotly debating the potential for the stock market to drop substantially. Speculation centered on the impact of a 500-point Dow Jones Indicator (DJI) drop in a single day. One member of the group was absolutely certain no such drop could occur. The next day the DJI dropped 506 points.

Under circumstances involving information and evidence conflicts, the truth becomes probabilistic. Interrogators often will start questions with: "Is it more likely . . . ?" "Is it highly probable . . . ?" "Is it virtually certain . . . ?" and "Are you absolutely certain . . . ?" *More likely* is better than 50 percent probability. *Highly probable* has to be specifically defined because it can range from the 50 percent or more of *more likely* to the 99 percent or more of *virtual certainty*. Questions about *absolute certainty* imply no realistic, conceivable situations exist in which the answer can be different from the one given. Experts should not use *possible* because it has no analytical foundation or mathematical meaning.

Remember, truth emerges from expert analysis activity and has weight in court because it is based on proven scientific methods and professionally recognized practices.

Credibility

Credibility emerges from an expert witness' professional knowledge of the specifics of the crisis situation and from qualifications which are based on education and experience. To preserve credibility, an expert witness must understand the core and limits of his or her professional knowledge. Over-extended expertise leads to loss of credibility and disqualification.[10]

Courts use expert witnesses to explain situations which are technically complex and require unique knowledge. Expert witnesses are normally qualified at the beginning of a trial. Formal qualification establishes initial credibility based on relevant edu-

---

[10] Attorneys often negotiate expertise and qualification boundaries with their experts to reduce costs and simplify presentation interaction.

cation, breadth and depth of experience, and organization or professional authority. Qualifications to testify as an expert witness are often the subject of sharp debate and even challenge via *voir dire*. If qualifications are undermined, an expert witness may not be allowed to testify or may be limited in ways that undermine the coherence of overall arguments.

> At the start of a trial, the defense attorney, a close friend of the judge, challenged the qualifications of a key expert. The plaintiff attorney, confronted with such courtroom politics, had difficulty qualifying his expert. The expert took the initiative and explained to the judge how his expertise reasonably and logically fit the situation. The judge accepted the expert's arguments and qualified him, resulting in a conference leading to a $425,000 settlement for the plaintiff.

It is important to establish expertise as well as qualifications. Qualifications are impressive, but demonstrated knowledge is convincing. Early in the adversarial dialogue, the expert witness should pick a question that shows the breadth and depth of expertise. The question used, however, should not deal with disputed issues because subsequent point/counterpoint interchanges may distract from the intent of the answer. In demonstrating expertise, an expert witness should be clear and brief yet comprehensive. Discipline is required to phrase answers in succinct sentences which are logically connected and contain only relevant information. Extraneous words dilute the impact of the response and undercut attempts to demonstrate expertise.

Credibility is often affected by little things. If examples are used, the expert witness should make sure they are commonly understood. Jargon or abbreviations specific to industry practice, government regulations, or academic theory should not be used unless they can be easily explained.

To sustain credibility, the expert witness must maintain the delicate balance between easy-to-understand and overly simplistic, potentially insulting answers. The expert witness who patronizes

Expert Witness Responsibilities

or talks down to an audience will be resented. The expert witness who respects others, and is in turn respected, knows most people can follow an argument if it is well presented and focuses on the main points.

Credibility is achieved situation by situation. Reputation is earned over the course of time.

The Result

In the courts of law and public opinion, most results derive from sensible and fair decision making by concerned individuals. Unfortunately, the decision-making process and the result are often difficult to prejudge. It is imperative the expert witness be objective, reasonable, and truthful. To support arguments and sustain credibility, the expert witness must be consistent and persistent and must believe success is possible.

Consistency

Prepared opening statements, the interrogation/testimony dialogue, and closing remarks should promote the key points of an argument. Where possible, the same words, phrases, and images should be used. Repetition may be boring to the expert witness, but it is the heart of consistency and essential to effectively educating a jury.

Notes, brief reports, and ready references may be used if permitted or when they will not be distracting. Such written information should be well organized. A shortage of time or lack of emotional stability may prevent careful sorting of disjointed or voluminous materials during adversarial exchanges. Caution should be exercised in the use of notes as strict adherence to a position can appear to reflect rigid, unreasonable thinking. Answers should be responsive to questions and to the changes they imply.

Consistency in communication drives home the point through repetition. Conversely, numerous excursions into secondary issues are disruptive because priorities and importance are blurred.

> *A television commercial for a headache medication was repeated constantly for a number of years. Individuals exposed to that commercial can still recall the medication, Anacin, even though the commercial has been off the air for a very long time.*

Persistence

In the battle to win the hearts and minds of the audience, persistence is critical to overcoming the diversions and distractions of the adversarial environment. Persistence ensures the message being delivered has a strong chance to be understood. Lack of persistence appears as weakness or evasion. Furthermore, it can signal there is little or no commitment to the argument.

> *During a trial by judge, an expert witness sensed the judge was confused by plaintiff claims regarding a head injury caused by incorrect placement of a door closure device aboard a ship. Expert witness answers under oath and the photographic evidence presented did not resolve the judge's confusion. The expert witness, however, noticed the courtroom had similar devices. He asked the judge if he could leave the witness stand for a moment and walked to a courtroom door. He showed the judge how the device disappeared behind the door when it was open, rather than into the passageway. The judge immediately understood the situation.*

Success and Winning

When all is said and done, the expert witness cannot guarantee a win. Some lawsuits, for example, are filed in the hope that sympathy for a client will overcome the truth of the situation. Some interrogators are more skillful in presenting favored arguments and undermining opposing testimony. Human beings can and do make illogical decisions in situations where emotions and images interact with facts and logical analyses.

An outstanding expert witness presentation does increase chances for success. Sometimes, however, success is clarifying the issues, contributing to understanding risk and minimizing loss, or saving individual reputations in an irrecoverable situation. The expert witness' ego should not be vested in the result, but in doing a good, comprehensive job under difficult circumstances.

The plaintiff attorney became totally absorbed by attempts to develop an accident explanation that would sell to a jury. He specifically hired an expert witness to diagnose the accident. In deposition, the expert witness was asked detailed questions about design and not about the accident. Unfortunately, the plaintiff attorney's focus on a winning accident explanation had undermined the expert witness' preparations. The presentation was an embarrassing failure.

Mistakes

Human beings make mistakes, and this makes life especially interesting in the interrogation/testimony situation. Errors of omission cause loss of important opportunities to make a point. Errors of commission cause the wrong or even opposite point to be inadvertently made. Probably the most common error is giving less than the best answer.

Errors, however, do create opportunities for all sides. An interrogator who discovers a mistake will almost certainly use it to undermine credibility. If an expert witness discovers a mistake, a relatively immediate and direct acknowledgment of the error can boost credibility. Error acknowledgment and correction are an indication of reasonableness, a desire to tell the truth, and competence.

Attempts to justify mistakes make an expert witness look foolish or deceptive, and give an exaggerated amount of time and attention to a weakness. Concerns about a mistake can be distracting and lead to additional errors. The expert witness should correct a mistake when discovered and move on.

In a trial exchange, an expert witness tried to justify conflicting statements in his deposition by claiming, "That is what I said but not what I meant." The attorney/expert witness exchange then broadened into other apparent, but not real, conflict areas. The jury became noticeably restless and uncomfortable.

Emotions

Emotions are part of the adversarial context, and they are used for effect by all parties. Fear, humor, anger, embarrassment and concern often are seen at trials and in television interviews. They are important elements in interest group forums and public hearings.

Fear

Stage fright is normal and is often useful in sharpening initial reactions and focusing attention on the issues at hand. Fear, however, causes the dry mouth, red face, shaking hand and wavering voice. A glass of water, a smile, and a deep breath can help overcome such physiological reactions. The expert witness should not squirm with discomfort, play with clothing or other items, or display personal habits that may be distracting or offensive.

Unreasoning fear is debilitating and almost certainly disqualifies anyone from participating in an interrogation/testimony dialogue unless forced to do so by law.

Humor

When the situation is extremely stressful, humor may be appropriate. Humor generally decreases tension if it is not sarcastic or flippant. Folksy analogies or parables can also work quite well to lighten the situation; however, jokes are usually not appropriate and may be offensive.

The expert witness should use humor cautiously and selectively if the intent is to decrease situation tension.

An exchange between a judge and an expert witness produced an unexpected lighter moment when the judge asked how a man fell and was severely injured. The expert responded that the injured party fell down one heck of a steep and hard three-story stairwell. The judge, who was a "good ole boy" from Tennessee, laughed and said, "You mean 'hell, not heck." The expert witness responded, "Whatever you want, sir, it's your court." The judge chuckled, appreciating this acknowledgment of his authority.

Anger

Anger implies the situation is already intensely negative. In angry situations, interrogators and expert witnesses give in to emotions and shouting and screaming occurs. Angry individuals, however, become upset and suspend effective listening. Mistakes and inadequate responses to questions often follow.

An opposing attorney was angrily attacking an expert witness. The questions were rapidly stated and nasty. The expert witness, who found himself becoming increasingly angry, discovered the attorney was really misstating the facts of the situation. Anger, therefore, was the attorney's tool to mislead and deceive. The expert witness, although strongly defending his positions, remained in control to prevent angry answers during deposition from becoming a stream of mistakes that could not be corrected in trial.

Juries or neutral audiences can interpret angry exchanges as the rantings and ravings of hotheads, thus reducing the credibility of both individuals. Anger expressed by an expert witness during a trial appearance is usually inappropriate for this reason.

An expert witness should consider using anger to increase tension only if there is nothing to lose. It may create an opportunity to adjust the situation more favorably after the behavioral chaos is resolved. An angry situation may lead to a temporary suspension of a deposition, giving time for a cooling off period during which existing positions can be reexamined and new issues studied.

Embarrassment

Embarrassment is often unavoidable, especially if a mistake is discovered. Embarrassment is not, however, inherently negative for it may generate sympathy for the embarrassed individual.

> *An elderly, gentlemanly expert witness with little trial experience made a mistake. The opposing attorney, an intense young man, unmercifully attacked him for the mistake. Under a brutal and withering cross examination, the expert witness broke down and cried on the witness stand. The jury saw the attack as unwarranted and vicious.*

Concern

Probably the most common reaction during a crisis is one of concern. The intense desire to both resolve the crisis and help the aggrieved parties is natural. Concern, however, must be tempered by objectivity to prevent misunderstandings from occurring.

> *The emotion-charged news conference by the president of the Union Carbide Corporation after the Bhopal chemical plant disaster that killed thousands of Indian squatters was compelling. But it conveyed a sense of personal and, therefore, organizational fault. Because of appearances, the Indian government angrily blamed Union Carbide for the disaster and threatened to arrest the Union Carbide president if he set foot on Indian soil.*

There is one final point regarding emotions. Expert witnesses often have a difficult time resisting the opportunity to advocate a pet position. Unfortunately, the advocacy of personal but marginal positions detracts from the key points that need to be emphasized in support of an argument.

Conflicts of Interest

There is a distinct difference between personal and professional interests. To be effective, an expert witness must be objective.

An expert witness who has a personal interest in a particular result has a conflict of interest.

Individuals who work as employees of an organization have a conflict of interest in interrogation/testimony situations. Opposing interrogators will quickly note this conflict to undermine the credibility of testimony.

Outside experts who are on contract to analyze and provide opinion are often treated as advocates even though there is little likelihood of a conflict of interest. It is important to remember that if a conflict of interest is discovered, disqualification may occur.

Counteracting Opposing Arguments

Interrogators regularly employ experts to develop questions, provide on-the-spot analyses, and create counter arguments. In legal situations, this activity may be privileged and, therefore, not discoverable. In other adversarial situations, failure to disclose can create the appearance of conspiracy and undermine objectivity.

Summary

The responsibilities of the expert witness were addressed in this chapter. The relationship between truth and credibility must be maintained. No expert witness, however, is responsible for a win. The best that can be done involves contributing to success through effective presentation.

Mistakes and emotions affect the adversarial dialogue. Mistakes must be dealt with quickly so that the expert witness' presentation is minimally affected. Emotions are unavoidable and affect tensions and stresses during the adversarial dialogue.

In the next chapter, discussion will focus on the interrogator's realm of questions and associated tactics.

Interrogators and Their Questions

Overview

Questions belong to the interrogator. Questions seek and provide information, focus conclusions and opinions, and create useful images. They can expose inadequate arguments or enhance good ones. Poor questions can give the appearance of incompetence or lack of preparation and undermine logic and reasonableness.

Interrogators often have favored, practiced interrogation approaches which they employ through a variety of tactics that probe, attack, and defend arguments, individuals and organizations.

Discussion in this chapter will first focus on interrogation tactics and games. Then the types of questions used by interrogators will be examined in terms of their intent and how they affect responses.

Interrogation Tactics

Interrogation tactics are employed to magnify the impact and effectiveness of questions. The expert witness who is trying to effectively represent the truth of a situation must remain alert to the win/lose implications of such tactics in the interrogation/testimony dialogue.

Theory to Reality

Theory, practice, and situation-reality questions are often deliberately intermixed by interrogators. To be effective, the expert witness must ensure that answers distinguish theory from practice, practice from situation reality, and situation reality from theory. If it is unclear what relationship is being questioned, clarification must be immediately solicited. Argument clarity and reproducibility result from successfully accounting for such questions. Argument confusion and, worse, the opportunity for an opposing interrogator to mix arguments intended for one purpose with arguments intended for a different purpose stem from a failure to keep an effective audit trail.

> At trial, an expert witness was confronted by the apparent physical impossibility of an answer he had given at deposition a year earlier. In trying to sort out what happened, he became more confused and his subsequent testimony began to unravel. A post-trial analysis revealed that the answer was essentially correct if it were related to business practices rather than theoretical abstractions.

Hard Ball and Soft Ball

"Hard ball/soft ball" is most often used by interrogators as a test of an expert witness' convictions and a mechanism to obtain unguarded disclosures. Essentially, an aggressive, unreasonable hard ball interrogator pressures the expert witness to defend a particular position. Hard ball challenges are periodically suspended so that a more reasonable soft ball interrogator can intervene.

Hard ball interrogation leaves nothing unchallenged. Definitions, concepts, methods, analyses, knowledge, experience and competence are all subjected to an uncompromising attack. Nothing is believed and there are no agreements with the answers. The soft ball interrogator restrains the hard ball interrogator by appearing to understand the expert witness' argument or by offering compromise and solace.

Interrogators and Their Questions

While hard ball/soft ball interrogators have different roles, their purpose is the same: to obtain information favorable to particular positions and to undermine opposing arguments.

Slow Down and Speed Up

The "Slowdown and Speedup" tactic is the equivalent of the "country bumpkin" interspersed with the "city slicker." The country bumpkin is somewhat slow-witted and dull. The city slicker is fast and smart.

The purpose of an interrogator's slowdown mode is to lull the expert witness into a sense of false security, cause distraction through boredom, and encourage progressively sloppy contradictory answers. Slowdown drains the tension from the adversarial dialogue and can drain the energy from the expert witness. Adrenaline surges sharpen answers but lead to rapid mental exhaustion. Slowdown exacerbates this latter effect.

Speedup suddenly gets to the crucial points or themes of the argument, and a distracted expert witness may find important questions have been asked and less than thoughtful answers given. While slowdown may account for 80 percent of the time, speedup accounts for 80 percent of what is important.

Questions as Answers

Asking questions in the form of a desired answer constitutes an attempt to limit debate. An interrogator asking such a question will often follow with a demand for a yes or no answer that is intended to eliminate the opportunity for the expert witness to address the subtle, complex aspects of a situation or to articulate conditional or counter arguments.

Individuals who have little interrogation/testimony experience often provide the yes or no answer because they are intimidated by the interrogator. The expert witness definitely should get the correct answer into the record regardless of the intensity or persistence of an interrogator's demand.

During a deposition, an opposing attorney tried to intimidate an expert into answering just yes or no. When the expert witness answered that the questions could not be answered in such a limited way, the attorney showed frustration and indicated the witness was not responsive. The expert witness indicated the attorney had the right to ask the questions, but that the witness had the right to provide the answers.

Definition Challenges

Challenges to definition are essentially assaults on the words and language used to communicate and educate an audience. If agreement is not reached on what is meant, the quality of the dialogue is degraded.

The expert witness must maintain control of the terminology used to define or describe theory, practice, and situation reality, and to note what constitutes a relevant or irrelevant shift in the meaning of words. Loss of definition control means the essence of an argument has been turned over to the opposition.

> During deposition, an opposing attorney questioned an expert witness about the nuances of the language used by engineers. The questions were quite precise, even soliciting answers that focused on, for example, the differences between a design analysis and the analysis of a design.

Repetition of Similar Questions

Questions are often repeated in the hope that they will solicit different answers or different behavior. The expert witness, therefore, must keep track of prior answers to ensure the potential for contradictions in testimony is minimized.

Repetitive questions can be boring and frustrating. Repetition, however, is an interrogator's way of testing an expert witness' memory and self control.

> One of television's most famous investigative reporting shows, "60 Minutes", is known to repeat questions to get the answer and image desired. A witness who gives in to

annoyance during an interview will almost certainly appear in the worst possible light when the show is presented.

Qualifications versus Knowledge

Challenges to qualifications were discussed previously. Nevertheless, even if an expert witness has been judged qualified, it is not unusual for an interrogator to attempt to undermine qualifications by questioning the breadth or depth of knowledge. In these situations, the expert witness should strongly affirm the relevance of knowledge applied to the reality of the situation. Failure to do so will not only undermine qualifications but credibility as well.

"Out-of-Context" Questions

"Out-of-context" questions take statements from the normal flow of a prior discussion and use them in a different context to imply a different meaning. The purpose is to undermine selectively the logic of a well-crafted argument and create the appearance of contradictions. Out-of-context questions may be a sign of desperation or indicate a lack of effective opposing arguments.

The expert witness must recognize that the questions are out of context and tell the jury what is occurring. An effective response to such questions involves first noting that the question takes a statement out of context. The expert must then provide an answer that defines what the actual context was, what was meant, and how the information should be used. An expert witness should keep the answer short and to the point to ensure the correct train of thought is clearly understood. The image thus created by the answer is one of interrogator deception and expert witness honesty.

Out-of-context questioning is a constant problem for any expert witness. The great majority of depositions contain numerous opportunities for even the best answers to subsequently show up out of context. It is, therefore, very important to read the source material for any quote before answering.

> An expert was advised that the opposing attorney was noted for using out-of-context questioning as his primary tactic during trial. The expert witness in preparing nearly memorized his deposition. When the out-of-context questioning occurred, the expert witness answered all such questions by saying, "That is out of context. We were discussing _____. Here is what was meant, and here is how your question misses the point." The opposing attorney was visibly shaken by the expert witness' performance and was unable to mount an effective cross examination.

Emotional Assaults

Shouting and screaming during the adversarial dialogue and threats that precede and follow it are increasingly common. Shouting and screaming shuts down dialogue and strongly indicates the expert witness, regardless of qualifications, has nothing worthwhile to say. Interrogators who employ this tactic substitute noisy emotions for reason in the hope that an audience can be favorably influenced by strength of conviction. Because shouting and screaming causes confusion and dismay, an expert witness may give a poor answer.

> In a deposition, an opposing attorney's shouting-and-screaming behavior was exceptionally discourteous and unprofessional. Questions which had no relevance to the situation were asked and simply heaped scorn on the expert witness. Some questions were screamed in such rapid-fire succession that answering became difficult and was almost certain to contain mistakes. The expert witness stopped the deposition and requested a magistrate be provided to control decorum. When the attorneys indicated this was not possible, the expert witness noted the situation on the record and demanded professional treatment.

Emotional tactics disrupt everyone's equanimity and it is important to take breaks when anger begins to surface. An expert should not persevere if the situation is so unsettling that mistakes will almost certainly be made.

Interrogation Games

The great majority of activities in the interrogation/testimony environment are legitimate. However, a variety of interrogator games are played outside normal boundaries and controls.

Threats

Threats generally take place off-the-record because on-the-record threats can be construed as an attempt to prejudice an expert witness' testimony. Off-the-record threats are attempts at intimidation, and an expert witness should not respond to such a threat unless physical confrontation occurs.

> *An expert witness was threatened during a restroom break. He reported the threats to the attorney who had hired him. The attorney subsequently grabbed the opposing lawyer by the throat, shoved him against the wall in front of witnesses, and counter-threatened him. Subsequent disciplinary actions were needed to resolve the situation.*

On-the-record threats do occur and usually focus on a particular business practice or employment. It is not unusual for such a threat to involve the prospect of an investigation, particularly involving the Internal Revenue Service.[11]

A threat is not necessarily negative. It may indicate the expert witness' argument is fundamentally sound and correct.

Deception

Misrepresentation of role and responsibility is all too common. The media, through investigative reporting, is constantly misrepresenting itself as common people seeking information or

---
[11] An expert confronted with a persistent on-the-record threat may have to obtain independent legal counsel to counteract this behavior.

help while their real motivation is to uncover illegal or unethical activity.

Role deception is not limited to the media. To obtain information about the other side that is not discoverable through due process, a few attorneys do misrepresent who their client is. Disclosures obtained through misrepresentation can bias, disrupt, and damage legal proceedings.

> *In one court case, an opposing attorney misrepresented himself as working for the expert witness' client. The deception was discovered by the expert witness who immediately requested a private meeting with a judge. To prevent deception from appearing on the court record, the case was settled.*

Rationalized Fiction

Sometimes the pressures of the adversarial environment cause people to create unsupportable versions of reality. This can occur by accident; however, an expert witness cannot condone or contribute to deliberate fiction in the interest of winning. If this occurs and is discovered, the expert witness' reputation will be damaged. Furthermore, even a won lawsuit can be overturned if an unreasonable version of reality is the basis for a jury's decision.

> *In an overly long predeposition preparation meeting, the attorney tried to nail down the details. Without realizing it, he essentially discounted the extensive preparation activity of his expert witness and created a testimony framework that was not technically accurate. In the deposition the next day, the expert witness was unable to resolve the dissonance between his own preparations and the attorney's extensive demands. The expert witness received constant criticism during each major break, and when the deposition was over, the attorney spent three hours debriefing him. The expert witness should have resolved the clash of wills and ideas prior to deposition.*

The expert who discovers rationalized fiction should suspend activity until the situation is resolved.

Deliberate Misquotes and Improper Quotes

Deliberate misquotes are an attempt to discover if the expert witness remembers what was said or is smart enough to ask. Often the misquote is a subtle shift in terms which creates a substantial shift in meaning. A deliberate misquote may also appear to be, or actually be, a simple mistake in reading by an interrogator. As mentioned earlier, an expert witness should personally examine the document from which any quote is taken to determine accuracy, context, and authenticity.

Sometimes improper quotes find their way into interrogations. This can happen when a confidentiality agreement, which is used to prevent the disclosure of court sealed documents, is leaked for future use. Unfortunately, such uses are very difficult to discover because the passage of time blurs memory or a quote can be slightly altered and, therefore, technically nonconfidential. If sealed information is used by either side, it may constitute contempt of court.

During a trial, an expert witness for the plaintiff became aware of a line of cross examination questions that could have come only from sealed records. At a break, the expert witness explained the situation to the plaintiff attorney and requested access to the judge. A quick conversation between opposing attorneys led to a sudden settlement.

Physical Deprivation

At times, the necessities of life are withheld to increase stress. The lunch that never arrives and the water pitcher that doesn't gets filled may constitute deliberate acts.

One favored deprivation ploy is to get an expert witness to answer just one more question before a break. There are invariably follow-up questions that can take many minutes to complete.

An effective expert witness strongly resists deprivation because it increases the likelihood of mistakes.

Admiral Hyman Rickover interviewed individuals scheduled to take command of a nuclear submarine by subjecting them to an intellectually rigorous, physically uncomfortable examination by senior officers assembled in his office. Command promotion was linked to reactions and performance under pressure.

Questions

Questions have specific and distinct motivations in the interrogation/testimony dialogue. Questions initiate dialogue and, therefore, support proactive behavior.

Questions are the basic tools of the interrogator.

"Why" Questions

"Why" questions are aimed at understanding and exposing the foundation of an opposing argument. Such questions request divergent thinking and often ask for information beyond already disclosed or anticipated testimony limits. Unexpected or surprise disclosures can result from such fundamental questions.

To minimize surprise, why questions should be answered by referring to prior stated positions, and should be based on relevant theory, practice, and reality. An expert witness should not speculate about why something happened. "I don't know why" may be the best answer because ignorance is recoverable through additional analysis effort.

One further note: Why questions may indicate the interrogator has not prepared and is, therefore, becoming educated. They may also indicate lack of understanding or inexperience.

"How" Questions

"How would this be done" questions invite on-the-spot design or development of products and processes. Such questions essentially ask that many weeks and months of analysis be done instantaneously. Through the use of how questions, interrogators can break down even the most carefully constructed responses. How questions can be strung together in a sequence that converges on and then exceeds the limits of an expert witness' knowledge. Such questions increase answer complexity and the likelihood of contradictions.

> *In a deposition, an electrical engineer was asked how he would design a switch to survive the marine environment. Some 50 questions later, he was forced to admit that his answers, while basically correct, did contain a number of contradictions. The switch, while simple in concept, became the opposing attorney's vehicle for undermining arguments and damaging credibility.*

When confronted with a how line of questions, an expert witness should indicate the inappropriateness of trying to do an extensive analysis under the time constraints and stresses of the interrogation/testimony dialogue. How questions should be strongly resisted but answers should contain an offer to do additional work.

There is one exception to the above. If an interview has specific time limits, an expert witness can discuss how in great detail. An interrogator is then pressured to cut off the answer to save time, and risks appearing impolite. Caution is indicated because excessive detail and minutia can confuse or bore an audience.

"What If" Questions

"What if" or hypothetical questions are related to crisis realities but introduce new ideas to obtain a different interpretation of the situation. What if questions test an expert witness' understanding of opposing positions and flexibility in dealing with change. Such questions can be answered by comparing and contrasting the existing "what is" position with the speculative "what if" position. This provides a strong answer firmly grounded in fact and analysis, and is credibility enhancing. An expert witnesses, however, has to be careful about answering hypothetical questions.

A young military officer participating in a career day activity was asked by a kindergarten student what would happen if poison gas got into the classroom. In blunt military fashion, the officer answered, "We will all die." The children became frightened, and the story made the news. He would have been more prudent to have answered, "This will not happen because the poison gas is sealed in a container in a guarded building on the other side of the mountain."

"What if," "what is," and "what should be" are at the heart of the differences between opposing sides. Plaintiff attorneys normally argue what should be or what should have been to convince juries that defendants could have produced a better product or service and, therefore, prevented an accident or crisis. Defense attorneys normally argue what is or what was reasonable at the time to diffuse plaintiff arguments of inadequate care. What if questions shift the ground between the plaintiff and defense positions.

Bind Questions

Bind questions have more than one interpretation or contain internal contradictions. Bind questions have no right or wrong answer, only better or worse ones. Bind questions often appear quite simple to an audience but can cause considerable confusion for the expert witness.

In the Iran-Contra hearings, Oliver North was asked whether he felt that dissent was somehow unpatriotic. There is, of course, a constitutional right to dissent, but dissent taken to extremes constitutes treason. There is no perfectly right answer.

Interrogators use bind questions to create confusion and the appearance of evasion. The expert witness can handle such questions by noting the inherent contradictions. A bind question can also be answered by restating the question as the answer. This approach is called mirroring.

Significant but Irrelevant Questions

Significant but irrelevant questions, first and foremost, have nothing to do with the subject at hand. Such questions amount to axe grinding, and are intended to create unfavorable images that compromise an expert witness.

> *During a television interview about the federal government's investments in high technology, an expert witness was asked how anyone could justify the expenditure of billions of dollars when people were homeless and starving. The expert witness became flustered and stumbled over subsequent topically relevant questions.*

An expert witness should indicate that significant but irrelevant questions are outside the scope of the inquiry. Furthermore, it is reasonable to answer that preparation, expertise, or authority is inadequate to compare and contrast these unrelated subjects.

Vague and Thoughtless Questions

Vague and thoughtless questions may indicate that the interrogator is grasping for ideas, pausing to collect thoughts, or poorly prepared. The simplest way to control such questions is to ask for clarification. A vague or thoughtless question will often be withdrawn because the interrogator does not know what was meant.

Truly stupid questions often are so illogical or ignorant they are disconcerting. The expert witness should not answer a stupid question because doing so amounts to an attempt to make sense out of nonsense. It is, however, appropriate to note the question does not make sense.

> *It is possible that stupid questions result from distraction. During a briefing on a research program, an expert witness was asked a question about legality. This question was not relevant to any aspect of the briefing and, as it turned out, was a mistaken leftover from a previous meeting. The expert, however, was nonplused and became confused.*

Some interrogators use poor grammar. Their questions are convoluted and ill conceived. It is important to have a clear question so subsequent interpretation is consistent with the intent of the answer. The expert witness should take the time to get a correctly worded question so there are no ambiguities.

Summary

The tactics, games, and questions that interrogators use in soliciting answers were addressed in this chapter. Interrogation tactics and games affect the quality of truth telling. Individual questions are the focus of the interrogation and different types of questions not only address different types of information but also have different motivations.

In the next chapter, discussion will focus on expert witness' answers.

Expert Witnesses and Their Answers

Overview

Answers belong to the expert witness. Answers derive from facts and analyses and lay out systematic and deliberate arguments. They provide succinct information, create clear images, leave a favorable impression, and effectively educate an audience. Poor answers are excessively wordy and complex. They are often illogical, speculative or unreasonably biased. They create confusing images that remain long after an interrogation/testimony interchange is complete.

Expert witnesses must uphold the truth with their answers. While they should be willing to represent a reasonable favored argument, they must recognize the strengths and weaknesses of all alternative arguments.

Discussion in this chapter will first focus on a variety of testimonial tactics and games. The types of answers provided by expert witnesses will then be examined in terms of their content and impact.

Testimonial Tactics

Testimonial tactics enhance the effectiveness of answers. They are not, however, as powerful as interrogation tactics because they are reactive rather than proactive. All such tactics must be employed within the boundaries of the inquiry environment and are limited by knowledge, expertise, and authority.

Disclosure Timing

The defense expert witness normally has the advantage of direct access to needed organization information and support. The plaintiff expert witness, on the other hand, may not have detailed knowledge of, or specific experience with, a particular product. Furthermore, he or she will not have information which is maintained in the minds of defendant personnel.

As a general rule, plaintiff expert witness depositions should follow defense expert witness depositions so that discovery is more complete and surprises are minimized. If possible, time between defense depositions and plaintiff depositions should allow for a reading of the transcript of defense expert witness depositions.

> *During a plaintiff expert witness' deposition, it became obvious that a substantial amount of discovery information was missing. Questions were constantly answered with the phrase "That information was not provided, even though it was requested prior to deposition." One crucial aspect of the deposition involved the appropriate industry and government standards used to underpin the development of a particular design. The issue was that a major industry/government conference regarding design had occurred either just before or just after the product was developed. The manufacturer was found to have designed to standards that existed before this conference. He did not place "what should have been" in the stream of commerce.*

Maintain Professionalism

An expert witness is a professional. Professionalism is supported by poised and reasonable testimony that is both truthful and consistent with objectives. Professional treatment, however, is not always granted and may have to be demanded when the situation is unprofessional.

The expert witness who is a permanent employee of an organization is in a unique professional situation. First, testimony serves both business survival and career stability needs. Second, organization advocacy is expected, and an interrogator will proceed accordingly. It is important, therefore, that the organization's expert witness be above reproach. (Evasion will be treated as deception.)

Outside contract professionals are often hired only for their ability to support crisis-related activities. In order to continue to practice, a contract professional must maintain a reputation as a respected and valued truth teller. It is professional for outside experts to provide a solid analysis, lend expertise in the development and conduct of testing, present logical and reasonable positions to an audience, and effectively handle the interrogation/testimony dialogue. It is unreasonable for an organization to expect such an individual to risk a hard-earned professional reputation in the interest of one special situation.

Defense of organization is the professional duty of the employee. Defense of profession is the duty of the outside expert.

Thoughtful Answers and Acknowledged Limits

There is a fine line between thoughtless and deliberate answers. All too often, an expert witness rushes to get an answer on the table so as not to appear evasive or unknowledgeable. Unfortunately, complex questions demand more thought than simple ones because there are a greater number of variables and, therefore, potentially correct answers.

An expert witness must craft an answer that is both an appropriate response to the question and to the multifaceted aspects of the interrogation/testimony dialogue. It is important, therefore, that the expert witness demonstrate the quality and strength of an argument and, at the same time, acknowledge its limits. Such an approach is reasonable and enhances credibility by distinguishing truth from speculation. It is important, however, to advise a client of this intention to acknowledge limits because this may disrupt strategic and tactical plans.

The Effective Expert Witness

An attorney was pursuing a lawsuit that had little merit. His intention was to have the expert write a report and to accept any settlement offer. The expert wrote a complete report and acknowledged the limitations of his investigation. The attorney asked the expert to remove the limiting phrases and sentences to provide a maximum-settlement opportunity. A negotiation eventually satisfied both the expert and the attorney.

Keep It Simple and Straightforward

The most effective expert witness makes complex situations easy to understand. Language is kept simple. Sophisticated technical concepts are dealt with in a straightforward step-by-step manner. Tendencies to expound upon minutia and ramble on to make the answer better are suppressed.

In a congressional hearing, an executive for a government agency was describing the benefits of a regulation on competition in federal contracting. The first 90 seconds of the answer were well articulated, even brilliant. The executive, however, decided he could make the answer better with just one more example. Unfortunately, the example triggered an hour-long debate on a related but essentially irrelevant issue. The value of his initial answer was lost, as was control of the agenda.

Making a Point

The easiest and most common way to make a particular point is to contrast the position supported with opposing alternatives and to explain why the avowed position is more reasonable.

The second most common way to make a point is to take a clear and strong position by listing the inherent pluses, and then pursuing this most favorable interpretation to its obvious conclusion. Nothing is said about the negative aspects of the position. Essentially, the weight of positive images, not reason, is expected to dominate in the minds of the audience.

It is also possible to make a point or gain attention through use of a creative phrase, analogy, or sound bite. Headlines and punch lines cause people to think.

The National Enquirer often has startling headlines about bizarre subjects. "UFOs Bring Race of Intelligent Frogs to Populate the Amazon," "Woman Gives Birth to Minotaur," and "Fountain of Youth Found in Trinidad," might be among the headlines. They are intended to grab the attention of a potential purchaser and to peak curiosity. An audience who can be made curious will give greater attention to an expert witness' arguments.

Finally, when making a point an expert witness should speak directly to the audience. This increases intimacy and is the equivalent of saying, "Listen to this, it is important to you in making your decision." Conversely, when deflecting a point, an expert witness should speak to the interrogator.

Testimonial Games

Because of the reactive posture of the expert witness, there are few opportunities to game the situation. Nevertheless, the following games do occur and can affect result.

Sloppy Preparation

It is all too easy to think that the situation is well understood and that additional preparation is a waste of time. Unfortunately, this assumption undermines an expert witness' ability to sharpen his or her focus and to deal effectively with the inconsistencies and surprises that are part of any crisis situation. An interrogator can use sloppy preparations to turn ignorance into stupidity, or inability to answer into insensitivity.

There is no real excuse for being unprepared other than that the crisis is ongoing, and there is literally no opportunity to prepare. In most instances, there is considerable time to review films, documents, evidence, test results, and reports. An expert who fails to review and organize information into useful and appropriate groupings immediately prior to testifying is acting irresponsibly.

There is one unique situation associated with preparation that needs to be addressed. Under certain circumstances, an expert witness' apparently sloppy preparation is really the fault of the individuals who are holding the information.

> *During deposition, an opposing attorney asked an expert witness a question that appeared to be inconsistent with available facts. At the break, the expert discovered that an important deposition transcript had been mistakenly or deliberately withheld. The expert witness resumed deposition testimony in an uncertain state, unsure about the prospects for other missing important information.*

Acting as Mouthpiece

Some expert witnesses will literally represent any position regardless of its reasonableness. Acting as a mouthpiece is somewhat understandable when the individual is permanently employed, but is almost never acceptable behavior for an outside expert witness. Mouthpiece behavior does everyone a disservice because it undermines an effective understanding of situation risks and the probability of success. Such behavior can and does damage an expert witness' reputation.

Misrepresenting Expertise

It is acceptable, at times, to stretch expertise into closely allied fields. The expert witness must, however, clearly note the risks associated with stretching expertise, and make suggestions to obtain more knowledgeable experts. By exposing professional limits, an expert witness supports the development of an effective analytical team.

Misrepresenting expertise undermines analytical and presentation effectiveness because it exposes the expert witness to disqualification or ridicule.

Taking Data for Other Purposes Without Disclosure of Intent

An expert may take data that is extraneous to the issue under consideration. Unless this is approved in advance, it is dishonest, costly and possibly confusing and counterproductive. The question that must be answered in taking more than obviously relevant data is "is this being done to ensure completeness so that additional testing is not necessary?" If the answer is not affirmative, then it should not be done.

Introducing Personal Interests into Agreed Position

An expert witness may let personal interests bias testimony. The rationalization for introducing personal interests in the interrogation/testimony dialogue is that it will not hurt the deliberations but may serve a useful purpose beyond the situation at hand. Unfortunately, personal interests are a distraction to an audience and may even constitute an inaccurate or incomplete understanding of overall technical or business practices.

> *Just prior to the taking of depositions in a civil suit, a respected engineering professor wrote a brief report that clearly represented a pet position on directing exhaust gases overboard from small boats. The pet position, which was appropriate for ships, was ridiculous when applied to small boats. The engineering implications were so deviant from practice or common sense that the expert on the opposing side advised his client the reputation of the professor would be irreparably damaged by cross examination. A successful attempt was made to settle the suit. This saved the dean from embarrassment and, at the same time, acknowledged that the case was lost.*

"Caving In" or "Selling Out"

The expert witness is responsible for good advice and an effective presentation of arguments. He or she should not "cave in" to the pressure to represent an illogical or unsustainable position, and should not "sell out" when opposing arguments appear to be overwhelmingly reasonable.

> *During breaks in deposition testimony, an expert witness was constantly pressured to use discredited information to support a favored argument. After one of many breaks, the expert witness resolved the matter by telling the truth in a simple and direct manner. His deposition testimony was subsequently used in court and became the basis for dismissal of the case. The ethics of the situation, however, are not perfectly clear. The expert witness was truthful but he sold out to the opposition.*

Answers

Unless time is predefined or limited, it is difficult to finish an inquiry or stop a line of questioning. Interrogators have the initiative and there are no certain ways for the expert witness to control the questions. There are no guaranteed answers that work every time (and possibly even most of the time). There are, however, reasonable answers that help direct inquiry, signal closure, or drain the energy from the interrogation/testimony dialogue.

Answers are the fundamental tools of the expert witness.

Lack of Knowledge

Lack of knowledge essentially closes a line of inquiry. Nobody knows everything or can instantly provide all the answers to complex questions. The expert witness should suppress the natural tendency to press on through ignorance as it leads to speculation and ineffective even wrong, answers. "I don't know" and an expression of a willingness to go further are satisfactory.

No Comment

"No comment" also closes a line of inquiry. It is not, however, based on lack of knowledge, but upon the presumption that any information disclosure is inappropriate or damaging. No comment answers give the appearance of evasion or insensitivity to situation.

Yes and No

Lots of yes and no answers without embellishment will drain energy from an interrogation. Yes and no reflect affirmation and negation but do not describe the reasons for their choice. The information deficit that results from such answers can end the interrogation or prompt the interrogator to start a more productive line of inquiry. The expert witness must be careful when answering questions yes or no because an interrogator may be phrasing a question to specifically limit an answer. Yes or no does not account for probability and may unduly bias conclusions or opinions by being too absolute in nature.

> *On the way to a deposition, a defense attorney asked his expert to answer as many questions as possible with yes or no. His intent was to minimize exposure and risk in a high profile case.*
>
> *The expert witness' subsequent testimony was almost entirely yes or no because the frustrated opposing attorney did not know how to change question tactics or the structure of the questions.*

Change the Subject

A folksy anecdote can be disarming. As such, it may trigger a change in the subject and even the direction of the questions. A folksy anecdote that is not well thought out, however, may confuse an audience, and can also be subject to interpretations not immediately apparent.

Human Concerns

During a crisis, the need for urgent action dominates discourse. If the individual interrogated is involved in resolving an ongoing crisis, a comment such as "I've got to get back to saving lives and property, fighting this fire, or cleaning up this mess" may be an appropriate way of ending an interview.

(Notice that the comment is action oriented and shows a commitment to normal human concerns and to crisis resolution.) No reasonable interrogator expects someone to talk when action is needed.

Time Pressure

Interrogators may be interested in only one sensational point and, if unchecked, will use all the available time on a line of questions that support a favored position. The expert witness involved in a time-constrained interview should closely track the time and insist on moving on when the interrogation becomes unduly repetitive or obviously biased. It is the expert witness' job to ensure that complete information is provided.

Time pressure has another implication. At the end of an interview or the day, people become concerned about other commitments. The pressure, therefore, shifts to the individuals most immediately confronted with having to make a travel connection or get to another appointment.

> *It is not unusual for interrogators to be under time pressure themselves. In legal situations, depositions are often scheduled sequentially and in a short span of time.*
>
> *An expert witness, aware of flight schedules, deliberately slowed the inquiry by speaking less hurriedly and giving answers wordier than necessary.*

Take a Break

It is both necessary and appropriate to ask for a break when physical or emotional discomfort increase the likelihood of a mistake. Although breaks may occur on a scheduled basis (as in the case of trial), it is important to base breaks during deposition on need rather than schedule. An expert witness should take a break every hour to hour and a half or before a new interrogator begins questioning. A break will prevent fatigue and provide time to reflect on the proceedings and to regain equanimity.

It may be necessary to take many more breaks during an especially intense or professionally degrading interrogation. Breaks consist of taking a drink of water, standing up to stretch, leaving the room, asking for the question to be repeated, waiting for an attorney to object, and pausing for an appropriate period of time when the question is complex. Stalling for time by providing mushy or useless answers is foolish.

Refuse Abuse

An expert witness should refuse to answer questions that are abusive. An interrogator, in the heat of battle, might not recognize or intend abuse. If this is the case, a comment off the record noting the situation constitutes a personal affront rather than professional challenge might change the situation. If abuse is intentional and must be tolerated, the expert witness should take numerous breaks to regain composure and should note the situation for the record.

Interview Completion

"The interview is over" signals time is up and there is nothing more to be discussed. This is particularly effective if the expert witness controls the situation and believes that the answers provided are solid, substantial, and complete.

One caution: The tendency to expand answers to get it right during the interview is, unfortunately, all too often complemented by a desire to unwind in context after an interview is over. Do not let unguarded but pertinent discussion continue beyond the interview.

Code Words and Phrases

The legal profession uses words and phrases in highly definitive and specific ways. It is very important that the expert witness be aware of such words and phrases because they can influence the outcome of a deposition or trial.

"Reasonable" reflects what is most probable based on the facts and analyses. More or less reasonable answers directly affect the strength or weakness of arguments.

"Foreseeable" deals with alternative decisions and courses of action. Foreseeable is "what should have been" as opposed to "what was." It is the basis for the disputes between plaintiffs and defendants.

"Common sense" is not expertise because it is anecdotal and based on belief. For conclusions and opinions to matter in a court of law, they must be based on expertise, not common sense. The subtle challenges so often experienced by the expert evolve out of this distinction.

> *During trial, a question was asked about the application of scientific method to fact-finding testing. The question caused confusion, and the expert witness responded that field testing was not strictly done in accordance with scientific method (even though it was). This statement invalidated all subsequent discussion of testing because the court reasoned that the testing, performed in support of plaintiff arguments, was based on common sense and was, therefore, unscientific. The case was subsequently dismissed by the judge.*

Individual jurisdictions have other terms with distinct legal meanings and must be accounted for during testimony. Although federal laws and codes are supposed to be applied uniformly, individual judges and regional interpretations vary considerably. Individual state codes are even more diverse. It is important for an expert witness to ask an attorney about unique uses of terminology and to obtain portions of legal codes that reflect the specialized definitions.

Summary

Within this chapter the tactics, games, and responses an expert witness uses in answering questions were outlined. Expert witness tactics and games are reactions to interrogator activity. They affect the quality of truth telling in much the same way that interrogator tactics and games do.

Individual answers deal with both the meaning and motivation inherent in questions. No pat answers exist. Fundamentally, the interrogator controls the initiative through questions.

In the next and final chapter, the important points made throughout this book will be summarized.

Final Remarks

Overview

An effort was made throughout this book to focus on the needs of the expert in dealing with an increasingly effective interrogation community. Attorneys, reporters, members of Congress, and interest group advocates have a substantial advantage in the interrogation/testimony environment. They have the initiative in the dialogue and a set of well-established interrogation tactics and questioning approaches. The expert, even though truthful, can be unsuccessful in promoting ideas and interests where communicating, educating, and image making are essential to audience understanding.

These final remarks are intended to emphasize the bottom line of effective expert activity and testimony.

Understanding the Picture Leads to Success

Each adversarial environment has associated with it a unique set of rules. The courts are ruled by form, the media by sensation, the legislature by election, and the interest group by selective advocacy. To compete effectively, the expert must be attuned to the demands of these environments and must use deliberate, systematic, and survival-oriented approaches to deal with them.

Success in the adversarial dialogue starts with objectives and the establishment of a strategy that allows crisis issues to be integrated into the flow of business. A crisis management strategy should support the gathering of information and the preservation of evidence, the development of tests and analyses that lead to a solid risk assessment, and ultimately, effective preparation for and participation in the adversarial dialogue.

At the heart of the interrogation/testimony dialogue is a competition of questions and answers. Tactics, as well as words, are employed to enhance dialogue impact. Unfortunately, intense pressure can cause individuals to act unreasonably and make mistakes.

The probability of a successful result is maximized when an expert witness' testimony enhances favored ideas, limits weaknesses, and exposes problems with opposing arguments. Nevertheless, there is no certainty of a win in a situation where decision-making belongs to others.

The Basis for Success

Thorough analytical and testimonial preparation, strong defense of the truth, and avoidance of speculation make an expert effective.

Truth is the foundation of the argument and the basis for expert witness success. Truth telling has positive consequences for an individual's credibility and reputation and for an organization's bottom line. Failure to tell the truth undermines most chances for success even when facts and analyses support a favored position. Truth is not independent of its telling. The images that surround it clarify, confuse, and prejudice. Consistency and persistence are needed to ensure that a clear and accurate message is presented.

Speculation corrodes and damages good arguments. It takes the expert beyond the facts, analyses, and realities of the immediate situation and into a realm of uncertainty. Speculation often introduces unpleasant surprises. Interrogators, however, have the right to ask hypothetical questions that invite speculation. An expert witness' answer should provide a reasonable and succinct distinction between the reality of the situation and the fiction of speculation.

Thorough preparation creates confidence. The knowns and unknowns will have been separated by analysis. Testing will have clarified various alternative explanations of the crisis. Prebriefs will have exposed the most relevant questions, suggested appropriate answers, and prepared the expert by simulating the interrogation/testimony dialogue. Thorough preparation may not be possible when a crisis is ongoing. In such a circumstance, lack of knowledge or discussion limited to the known facts are appropriate and realistic.

Responsibilities

For better or worse, an effective testimonial presentation ultimately rests in the hands of the expert witness. Interrogators will challenge, confuse, and cause mistakes to occur. The expert witness must rise to the occasion by communicating in clear and understandable terms.

The expert witness must stay focused on the message to ensure the audience is educated. Argument strengths must be effectively represented and limits acknowledged in a reasonable and objective way.

Images are compelling and affect the outcome. Data handling, diagnostic and communication technologies, therefore, provide increasingly powerful analytical and presentation tools for the knowledgeable user.

Focus on the Question at Hand

The ultimate focus in the interrogation/testimony dialogue is the question and the answer, and what each means to an audience. The interrogator must ask the questions, the expert witness must provide the answer, and the audience must make a judgment. The expert witness must strive to present an effective answer to the question at hand using all of the tools, preparations, and skills available. The truth, after all, is built question by question and answer by answer.

Index

A

Analysis 44-47
  analytical results 46
  challenges to 47
  definition of 44
  general practice 45
  methods and results 46
    qualitative 46
    quantitative 46
  scientific theory 44-45
  situation reality 45-46
Analytical process flow (figure 1) 32
Analytical processes used 31-49
Answers 112-15
  break, take a 114
  human concerns 113
  interview completion 115
  knowledge, lack of 112
  no comment 112
  refuse abuse 115
  subject changes 113
  time pressure 114
  yes and no 113
Answers of expert witnesses 105-17
Audience, interrogator, and expert witness 65-75
Audiences 66-70
  friendly 68
  neutral 67
  tendencies and limits 69-70
  unfriendly 68-69

B

Basis for success 120-21

C

Caveat emptor, contradiction of 7-8
Challenge objectives 53
Code words/phrases 115-16
  common sense 116
  foreseeable 116
  reasonable 115
Communication and analysis activity not separated 29
Communication central 28-29
Conflicts of interest 88-89
Congress 16, 18, 52, 119

Congressional 3, 18, 108
Corporate personnel 17
Corporate representative 17, 28
Corporation 60. *See also* Organizations: and adversity
Credibility 81-82
Crises 18-19
   action team 15, 23-26, 29
   anticipated 21-22
   initial investigation team 23-24
   test and analysis team 25
Crisis control 33
   preservation 33
   resolution 33
   restoration 33
Crisis management 15, 17, 20-27, 30, 33-34, 48, 51, 53-54, 120
Cultural and regional conflicts 16
Cultural diversity 6

D

Damage control 51
Decision making 49
Deposition 16, 47, 57-58, 106, 114-15
Diagnostics 13
Disruptiveness 62

E

Early warning system 22
Emotions 86-88
   anger 87
   concern 88
   embarrassment 88
   fear 86
   humor 86

Environment characteristics 15
Ethics 8, 14, 111
Expert witness 72-74
   controls the answers 73
   influence of 74
   questions not controlled 73-74
   responsibilities of 77-89
Expert witness, preparation of 51-63
   don't assume knowledge 54
   facts and analyses 57-58
   information, gaining command of 56
   know the interrogator 59
   know the objective 51-52
   know the role 54-55
   prepared positions 57
   reason for appearing 55
   situation orientation 57
   visual aids 58
Exxon Valdez 32

F

Fact-finding testing 13, 37-39, 59, 116
Figure 1, analytical process flow 32
Figure 2, relationships between testing 39
Figure 3, relationship between objectives, knowledge, roles and reasons 56
Figure 4, interaction between interrogator and expert witness 72
Focus 121

Index

H
Human message 74

I
Industry standards 35
Information and evidence handling 34-36
  credibility and reputation damaged 34
  crisis, cause of 35
  organization information 34
  situation-specific evidence 35
Initial investigation team 23-25, 53
Interaction between interrogator and expert witness (figure 4) 72
Interrogation, definition of 1-2
Interrogation games 97-100
  deception 97-98
  deliberate misquotes/improper quotes 99
  physical deprivation 99-100
  rationalized fiction 98
  threats 97
Interrogation tactics 91-97
  definition challenges 94
  emotional assaults 96
  hard ball/soft ball 92-93
  qualifications versus knowledge 95
  questions as answers 93
  questions, out-of-context 95
  similar questions, repetition of 94
  slow down/speed up 93
  theory to reality 92

Interrogation/testimony trends 5-14
Interrogator 70-72
  answers not controlled 71
  controls the questions 70-71
  not the audience 72
  questions 91-104

L
Legal versus public relations staffs 26
Legislators 16
Long-term investment decisions 29

M
Media 9, 17-19, 26, 52-53, 57, 62, 97-98, 119
Media interviewers 9
Miniaturization 12
Mistakes 85
Money and time needed 29

O
Opposing arguments, counteraction of 89
Organizations 15-30, 107
  and adversity 19
  corporate management plans 21
  crisis management plans 21
  early warning system 21-22
  objectives 20
  strategy 20
Outside experts 27
Overview 1-3

125

P

Performance 11
Prebriefs 59-61, 121
  chit chat 61
  mock interviews 59
  murder boards 60
Predeposition 98
Prejudicial thinking 36
Preparation 2, 15-30, 56
  sloppy 109-10
Presentation 77-80
  communicator 78
  educator 79
  image maker 80
Pressure, being under 66. *See also* Stress
  of adversarial environment 66
  of testifying 65-75
Public disagreement 28
Public relations 26

Q

Questions 100-04
  bind questions 102
  "how" questions 100-01
  significant but irrelevant questions 103
  vague/thoughtless questions 103
  "what if" questions 101-02
  "why" questions 100

R

Relationship between objectives, knowledge, roles and reasons (figure 3) 56

Relationship between testing (figure 2) 39
Relationship between truth and credibility 80-83
Remarks, final 119-21
Responsibilities 121
Result 83-85
  consistency 83
  persistence 84
  success and winning 84-85
Reviews 47
Risk assessment 47-48

S

Societal conflict 5-6
Societal situation 14
Stage setting 61-62
Strategy 120
Stress 1, 65, 96, 115
Successful outcome 32-33, 84-85
Systematic thinking 33

T

Team cohesion
  outside experts and organization employees 27
Technological change 5
Technological considerations 9-13
  communication technologies 9
  computer simulation 10
  data-handling technology 11-12
  diagnostic technology 12-13
  laboratory investigation 13
Test and analysis team 25-26
Test techniques 39-44
  cameras, video/still 42
  checklists 41

field instrumentation 42
laboratory instrumentation 43
plans and procedures 40-41
predefined data recording forms 41
site orientation 40
Testimonial games 109-12
  caving in 111-13
  disclosing unauthorized data 111
  misrepresenting expertise 110
  mouthpiece, acting as 110
  personal interest 111
  selling out 111-12
  sloppy preparation 109-10
Testimonial tactics 105-09
  acknowledged limits 107
  disclosure timing 106
  making a point 108-09
  professionalism needed 106-07
  simple and straightforward 108
  thoughtful answers 107
Testimony, definition of 2
Testing 36-39
  fact-finding 37
  reconstructive 38
  types of 37
Trends 5-14
Truth 80-81, 104, 120-21

U

Understanding 119-20

W

Win/lose mentality 7

Give the Gift of
The Effective Expert Witness
to Your Colleagues

CHECK YOUR LEADING BOOKSTORE OR ORDER HERE

❏ **YES**, I want _____ copies of *The Effective Expert Witness* at $49.95 each, plus $5 shipping per book (Virginia residents please add $2.25 state sales tax per book). Canadian orders must be accompanied by a postal money order in U.S. funds. Allow 15 days for delivery.

❏ **YES**, I am interested in having Dr. Robert Warren speak or give a seminar to my organization. Please send information.

My check or money order for $_____ is enclosed.
Please charge my ❏ Visa ❏ MasterCard

Name _____

Phone _____ Fax _____

Organization _____

Address _____

City/State/Zip _____

Card # _____ Exp. Date _____

Signature _____

Please make your check payable and return to:
Gaynor Publishing
P.O. Box 462
Lightfoot, VA 23090

Call your credit card order toll free to: (888) 484-7750
Fax: (703) 250-4068